Praise for R

The sense of wonder and adventur Cowley's engaging account is palpable. Travel is one of the great educators and there is no more exciting and effective way of learning than through experience. At a time when ministers would have our children do little more than sit in a classroom, *Road School* suggests an alternative which is every bit as valid and powerful as conventional learning.

**Dorothy Lepkowska-Hudson,
freelance journalist and writer**

Cowley's *Road School* is an entertaining, accessible and practical guide to home education on the road.

Fiona Nicholson, home education consultant

Road School is a rip-roaring romp through Europe and China. It is not only the story of a family, which kept me chuckling out loud, but also a reflection on both parenting and education and politics today.

Anyone who teaches, and anyone who has a family of their own, will enjoy this book – not just for the entertainment value, but also for Sue's insights into what is really important when you work, and live, with children.

This book is an inspiration. I might not be off for six months, but I am certainly eyeing my suitcases with a glint in my eye and a bit more bravery.

Nancy Gedge, consultant teacher

Road School is an inspirational and lyrical journey, offering the reader a unique approach to home schooling on the road. Crossing continents with her partner and children, Sue describes how it is possible to offer an exciting and enriching curriculum, which eclipses conventional schooling by travelling and exploring the world. Any parent or teacher who reads this book will find themselves imagining life on the road with their children and many will adopt this approach. It is a magnificent book, which will start an educational revolution, mirroring Sue's awe-inspiring angle on education.

**Mike Fairclough, Head Teacher,
West Rise Junior School and author**

Road School

Learning through exploration and experience

Sue Cowley

Crown House Publishing Limited

www.crownhouse.co.uk

First published by

Crown House Publishing Ltd
Crown Buildings, Bancyfelin, Carmarthen, Wales, SA33 5ND, UK
www.crownhouse.co.uk

and

Crown House Publishing Company LLC
PO Box 2223, Williston, VT 05495
www.crownhousepublishing.com

British Library Cataloguing-in-Publication Data
A catalogue entry for this book is available
from the British Library.

Print ISBN 978-178583114-0
Mobi ISBN 978-178583191-1
ePub ISBN 978-178583192-8
ePDF ISBN 978-178583193-5

LCCN 2016959031

Printed and bound in the UK by
Gomer Press, Llandysul, Ceredigion

For the real life 'Frank', 'Alfie' and 'Edith'.

The world is a book, and those who do
not travel read only one page.
Anon

Contents

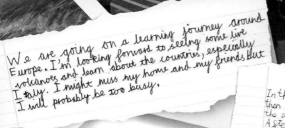

We are going on a learning journey around Europe. I'm looking forward to seeing some live volcanoes and learn about the countries, especially Italy. I might miss my home and my friends but I will probably be too busy.

In the morning we woke up at 6 o'clock then we got dressed. At 7 o'clock we got in the car and 3 hours later we arrived in Dover. After that we got on a big boat and it was very rocky. We went outside to look for birds but we didn't see any.

England

Very soon we are going on a road trip around Europe. I'm really excited about going to Italy to see the Last Supper. I hope we don't get into arguments while we are in the car. It's going to be fun!

Today we set off on our Learning journey. First we prepared everything and then drove to Dover. I'm writing my first diary entry on this cross channel ferry. Once the boat starts to move we will sail for an hour and a half across the English channel. The distance from Dover to Calais is 25 miles.

Ready to Go

'I want to go travelling,' I said, sliding a copy of *The Rough Guide to Europe* across the dining room table to where my partner Frank was sitting. Frank caught the book and looked up from his laptop. He had a spreadsheet open and he was tapping numbers into it. The spreadsheet had the title: 'Household Expenses'. Radio 5 Live was playing in the background.

'Huh?' Frank said, shaking his head. 'Like a holiday, d'you mean?'

'No, not a holiday,' I said. 'Proper travelling. Where you leave home and you don't come back for months on end. That kind of travelling.'

'And how would we pay for this?' Frank entered some more numbers into his spreadsheet. Frank's an accountant. He likes to know how much everything will cost. (It's a good thing somebody in our family does.)

'It's the ideal time to do it,' I said, leaning over to turn down the volume on the radio. I wanted to explain my reasoning as fast as possible. If QPR scored a goal in the match I was dead in the water. I had my speech all prepared.

'The kids are at the perfect age,' I said. (Our son Alfie had just turned 11; our daughter Edith was 8.) 'Alfie gets to avoid the whole Year 6 "endless months of preparing for SATs" thing. And Edith is a bright spark – she'll love the adventure. Plus, once they start secondary school we'll be stuck in England for the next eight years at least. And, as an added bonus, we get to spend lots of time with our children.'

'I don't want to spend lots of time with my children,' Frank said.

When I was a child my parents had a VW camper van, and one summer we went on tour in it. Thinking back, this happened shortly before they got divorced, so maybe there was a correlation between the two events. On our trip we toured around France, Switzerland and Italy. Quite how my parents managed to do this without the

Internet, the euro, TripAdvisor or the EU, I have no idea, but my memories from that holiday are still vivid, forty years later. This was the kind of adventure I wanted to recreate for our kids: strange new places, dusty tracks, exotic smells, the magic of exploration and the open road.

Frank typed a few more numbers into his spreadsheet, sighed deeply, then looked up and finally met my eyes.

'Is this even legal? Aren't they meant to be in school all the time or we get put in jail?'

'Home schooling isn't illegal, Frank. Not yet, anyway. We can teach them on the road,' I said. 'Or, rather, the road can teach them.'

'You mean *you* can teach them.' Frank scratched his goatee. 'You didn't answer my question about who pays for it. Travelling costs money. We can't work if we're travelling.'

'It wouldn't have to be expensive,' I shuffled in a bit closer to him and draped my arm across his back. 'We could both take a bit of time out. I was thinking we could hire a camper van. It would be romantic. And I could write a book about it. That way it would be tax deductible.' (Frank finds it very seductive when I talk about things being tax deductible.)

'I'm six foot five,' Frank said. 'I don't do camper vans. Can you imagine trying to drive a motor home into the centre of Rome?' He paused for a moment. 'No camper vans. And I want to fit in a visit to China. I've always fancied going to China.'

'Is that a yes?' I could hardly believe it.

Frank sighed again. It was the deep, long, heavy sound he makes when he is resigning himself to one of my crazy ideas.

'It's a yes,' he said, turning up the radio again to show that we were done. 'I guess that us going travelling is better than you having an affair, buying a fast car or learning to ride a motorbike. I think I'd better start a new spreadsheet. I'll call it "Midlife Crisis".'

Everybody Wants to Rule the World

'If we're going to do this, I want to go to India, China and Japan,' Frank said. 'Oh, and South America.'

'You're ambitious.' We were arguing about the route for about the millionth time. 'I was thinking more a road trip around Europe, finishing up in Paris. Then maybe a week in South America.'

'I'm *definitely* not going to Paris,' Frank shook his head as though he had a bug in his ear. 'I've been there too many times already. Don't you remember when we were in our twenties and Tom lived there? We used to visit him all the time.'

'My main memory of those days is of getting drunk and staying up until dawn, Frank,' I sipped my tea. 'That wasn't exactly the kind of visit to Paris I had in mind.'

Frank made a harrumph sound. 'I did the Interrail thing around Europe when I was a teenager. I've got some great stories about that. Mind you, it's probably best if you don't put those in your book. I'd like to go back to Germany, though. See the places where I spent time as a child.'

'Well, if we're going to India, China, Japan and South America, I'd really like to go to Malaysia or Indonesia,' I said.

'Japan sounds good. How about Brazil?'

'Yes, North America too. And Hawaii. I've always wanted to visit Hawaii.'

A week later we had argued about the route another million times. I had communed with Google and I had the ammunition I needed.

'Okay,' I said to Frank. 'I've got some figures for round-the-world flights taking in Malaysia, China, Japan, Hawaii and Brazil.'

'And?'

'And it comes to £3,832.27.'

Frank smiled. 'That sounds doable.' He began to tap some numbers into a spreadsheet.

'Each.'

'Ah.' His fingers stopped tapping. 'A road trip around Europe it is, then.'

'We should do one other destination. We've already been to India, Hawaii is too far and too expensive, and South America is full of poisonous bugs.'

'Like I said before, I've always fancied going to China.'

And that was that. Finally. Decision made. Destinations chosen. Now all we had to do was make it happen.

Bright Side of the Road

The kids were in the living room, collapsed on the sofa, watching TV after a long day at school. They were trying to munch their way through a packet of chocolate chip cookies before we noticed. We were pretending not to notice the disappearing chocolate chip cookie trick, because we had something much more important to talk about. I cleared my throat and made the announcement.

'We're taking you out of school.'

'Yay, cool,' Edith glanced up at me for a moment and then returned her gaze to the TV.

Frank came to stand beside me in a show of fatherly solidarity. 'We're going to go travelling around Europe, and then after that we'll fly to China. We'll be on the road for six months. Isn't that exciting?' he said.

'Yeah, great,' Alfie said. His eyes were still on the TV.

'We're going to learn through exploration and experience,' I said. 'No timetable. No SATs. No uniform. No teachers. No limits. We're going to educate you ... on the road.' I'll admit that my voice broke with emotion a bit at that point. I thought I was doing a good job of selling the dream.

'Sure, whatever,' Alfie said. He shrugged.

'You're a teacher, mummy, so there will be teachers,' Edith pointed out.

'She doesn't count,' Alfie said.

'Yes she does.'

'No she doesn't.'

'Yes she does.'

'No she doesn't.'

'Thanks kids.' Their level of enthusiasm wasn't exactly inspiring.

'Aren't you excited?' Frank wanted to know.

'Yes! We're really excited!' the kids shouted.

'Now can you be quiet?' Alfie said, exasperation in his voice. 'We're trying to watch *South Park*.'

Breaking the Law

The pages of my little black Road School notebook were filling up fast with lists of places to visit, museums and art galleries to see, hotels to book, things to pack. And rules. There had to be rules. You can take the teacher out of the classroom, but you can't take the classroom out of the teacher.

'We're going to need some rules for Road School,' I said as I scribbled another note in my notebook.

'What is it with teachers and rules?' Frank was typing some numbers into yet another spreadsheet. I looked over his shoulder. The title of the spreadsheet was 'Petrol Prices: Europe'.

'What is it with accountants and spreadsheets?' I stuck my tongue out at him.

'Why do we need rules? We're not exactly the rules oriented kind of people.'

'Rules are important. Rules help to create the right environment for learning. It's not just a free-for-all. These kids are going to need rules.'

'If you want rules, you go ahead and make some up,' Frank said. 'Just don't expect me to follow them.'

'Or us,' the kids piped up from the sofa.

'How about if I make up some rules that we will all like?'

'Doesn't that kind of defeat the object?' Frank asked.

'No one likes rules, mum,' Alfie said. 'That's why schools have them.'

'I think you'll like these rules,' I said. 'Why don't you just listen and see what you think? Turn off the TV for a minute.' I grabbed the remote and paused *South Park*. 'You really shouldn't watch this stuff anyway.'

'Aww mum!' Alfie said.

'That's our favourite episode of *South Park*,' said his little sister. 'It's the one where they go to an aqua park and end up swimming through a tsunami of urine.'

'Just give me five minutes.' I held up my notebook and tried to read my scrawled handwriting. 'Here you go. The First Rule of Road School is that we are on the move – the only constant is change.'

'Very poetic,' Frank said. 'What does it even mean?'

'That's not really a rule, mum,' Alfie said. 'It's more a statement of fact. Obviously we're going to be on the move, because otherwise it wouldn't be called Road School. It'd be called Staying At Home School.'

'I like the first rule, mummy,' Edith said, smiling at me. 'Especially the changing constantly bit. That's great.' I think she was just trying to make me feel better.

'Can I continue?' I said. They all nodded and Frank made a 'get on with it' signal with his hand. 'The Second Rule of Road School is that we hunt for interesting things – we are looking for learning.'

'I'm interested in learning about guns and volcanoes,' Alfie said.

'I'm interested in learning about Leonardo da Vinci,' Edith said.

'I'm interested in lunch,' Frank said.

'Noted. Can I continue?' I'm not going to lie and tell you they looked particularly enthusiastic about my rules, but I was on a roll

now and I was damn well going to get through them.

'The Third Rule of Road School is that you have to write a page in your diary every day. I got you these,' I said, holding up two hard-back A4 lined books.

'I don't like rule number three,' Edith said.

'Me neither,' Alfie agreed.

'Tough,' I said.

'Why do you have to ruin our trip with writing?' the kids whined.

'Because it'll keep the authorities off my back,' I said, 'Plus you'll thank me when you're older and you have it as a memento. You can stick tickets, maps, postcards and all sorts of things in your diaries as well. It'll be a brilliant record of what we did.'

'I don't have to keep a diary, do I?' Frank said.

'No you don't, Frank, because you're old already.'

Frank gave me a look. 'So are you,' he said. Then he muttered something under his breath that sounded suspiciously like 'bloody midlife crisis'.

'Is that the last of the rules, mum?' Edith said, stifling a yawn and looking longingly towards the TV, where Kyle was paused in mid-stroke as he swam through a giant pool of pee to hit the emergency release valve.

'Last one,' I said. 'The Fourth Rule of Road School is that some rules were made to be kept, but some rules were made to be broken. We just need to figure out which rules to follow and which ones to break.' I was pleased with this rule. Road School meant no uniform, no timetable, no government tests, no detentions, no homework. We were breaking the rules, right, left and centre.

'Now this rule I like,' Frank said. 'This is a rule I can live with.' Frank likes to think of himself as a bit of a rebel, although I'm not convinced that a desire for rebellion and a love of spreadsheets are natural partners.

'Hey, dad!' Alfie said. 'I've got a great idea!'

'What's that?'

'I'm going to apply rule number four to rule number three. That way I don't have to do any writing.'

'Great plan,' Frank said.

'Good idea, Alfie! I'm going to do that too,' his sister joined in.

'Well, that's just perfect,' I said. I tore the page of rules out of my notebook, screwed it up into a ball and threw it in the bin. 'You *have* to write in the diaries. That rule is not up for negotiation.'

'Dictator,' Frank said.

'Tyrant,' Alfie said.

'Meanie,' Edith said.

'Thanks for the compliments.' I snapped my little black notebook shut and handed the remote control back to the kids. 'But you can just call me mum.'

Heroes

The moment she learned that we were going to be travelling around Europe, Edith became obsessed with Leonardo da Vinci. She was interested in him before she found out about our trip. She had a library book from school about Leonardo that she read over and over again. Now she wanted to read every book ever written about him, visit everywhere he ever lived and see every painting, sculpture and model he ever made. It was pure, unadulterated child-like curiosity, fired up by an interest in *something*. Why does the education system stop us sustaining this feeling in kids? I was hoping that our road trip would help me to figure this out.

'Leonardo was born in Vinci,' Edith said. 'So obviously we have to visit Vinci.'

'I'll put it on the list,' I said, scribbling in my notebook.

'We have to see the *Mona Lisa*,' she added. 'That goes without saying.'

'I've already told your mum – I'm not bloody going to Paris,' Frank said, looking up from his spreadsheet. 'I've been there a million times already.'

'We've got to take them to Paris, Frank,' I said. 'You can go for a long lunch while we go up the Eiffel Tower and visit the Louvre.' Frank made a sound that was somewhere between a snort and a huff. I made another note in my notebook.

'Anywhere else, Edith?' I should really have kept my mouth shut at that point.

'*The Last Supper*,' Edith announced. 'We definitely must see *The Last Supper*. It's Leonardo's greatest masterpiece, alongside the *Mona Lisa*. Where's that one?'

'I think it's in Milan. I'll check now.' I opened my laptop and fired up Google.

Unless you've ever tried to visit *The Last Supper*, you'll have no idea how difficult it is to visit *The Last Supper*. You might imagine that you could just roll up in Milan, pay your entrance fee and go in to see it. But you'd be wrong. Instead, you have to book a slot for your visit by calling a phone number in Italy. When you call the phone number in Italy it is permanently engaged. When you eventually get through and talk to the woman in the ticket office, you have to nominate a specific day and time to visit. But you can't choose just any day or time. You must nominate one of only a few fifteen minute slots that are available, several months in the future.

During her reading, Edith was particularly entranced by the notion that, on some days, da Vinci would stare at his unfinished painting on the refectory wall for many hours, before adding a single brushstroke and going home for the day. Unfortunately, Leonardo decided to use an innovative new technique for his painting, and literally as soon as he had finished it, it began to deteriorate. Over the centuries various restoration methods have been used, and the latest restoration took twenty-two years. Yes, that's *twenty-two years*. It's no wonder they wanted to limit access to the thing. It took Leonardo several years to paint his masterpiece and, by the time I eventually made the reservations, it would feel like it had taken a similar amount of time to book to see it.

'It looks like it's quite tricky to get tickets,' I said to Edith. 'Do you really, really, really want to see *The Last Supper*?'

'Yes. Definitely.' She did a little flounce of her head to indicate that it was not up for debate.

There were lots of ways we could have planned the timing of the European leg of Road School. We could have gone with the flow and just seen what happened. We could have given ourselves a specific number of days to spend in each location. We could have spent a week in each different country that we visited. But, no: in the end it turned out that our Road School schedule was based around our daughter's burning desire to see *The Last Supper* by her hero, Leonardo da Vinci. And this meant that we had to be in Milan at 10.15 a.m. on Thursday 15 May. I seriously hoped that it was going to be worth it.

Born to Run

An early morning mist drifted along the river and seeped over the fields towards our house in a Somerset valley. It was 7 a.m. on a morning in early spring. The sky was clear and blue, although there was a chill in the air. The kids were in the car. The grown-ups were in the car. Everyone had been to the toilet. This was it then: we were setting off on our big adventure. Road School was Go.

'Have you got the passports?' I just wanted to be sure.

'You've asked me that twice already,' Frank said. 'Did you pack enough tea bags?'

'Yes. You've asked me that already. Let's go then. We don't want to miss our boat.'

'I'll go and get a few more tea bags, just in case.' Frank got out of the car and disappeared back inside the house.

I heaved a sigh and leaned over to check that Frank had indeed put four passports into the side pocket of the driver's door. Then I turned around to check on the kids. They were plugged into their games consoles, busy digging into the pile of snacks on the seat between them. The scent of Quavers hung in the air. The DVD player was showing *Cloudy With a Chance of Meatballs*. Again.

'It's going to be a very long day, and those snacks need to last you the whole way to Amsterdam.' I used my best teacher voice for the warning.

The kids carried on tapping on their devices and munching on the snacks as though I hadn't spoken. I sighed again. 'I don't know what is keeping your father.'

Edith looked up from her screen. 'Are we going to miss our boat?'

'No, it'll be fine. No need to worry.' I chewed on a nail.

There was the sound of the front door slamming and the key turning. Frank reappeared carrying a massive carrier bag. He opened the door, leaned into the car and dumped the bag on my lap.

'Here you go,' he said. 'I got a few more tea bags. Just in case. Better safe than sorry when it comes to tea bags.'

I sighed and bit my tongue. 'Finally. Great. Thank you so much.' I'd spent hours the night before carefully packing the boot so that all the bags went in and I didn't have to balance stuff on my lap during the journey.

'There's no need to get all uptight about it,' Frank said. 'I can put them in the boot if you like.'

'Can we just go?' If I let Frank loose in the boot now there would be an avalanche of suitcases. 'There might be traffic, and we don't want to miss the ferry.'

'Are we going to miss our boat, mum?' Edith piped up again.

'No, we are *not* going to miss our boat,' Frank said. 'I don't know why you're getting so stressed already. We've got six months of this. If you're stressed now, you won't make it past the first week.'

Alfie looked up from his games console. 'Mum, did you bring an adaptor?'

'What did you say? *What did you say?*' I'll admit that I was grinding my teeth by this stage. 'Don't you know we're running late? Don't you know we've got a ferry to catch? Don't you know they have shops in Europe?'

'There's no need to shout, mum,' Alfie said. 'Like dad says, if you're this stressed now, you won't make it past the first week.'

'Remember, mum,' Edith had a smile on her face, 'keep calm and carry on.'

'And don't forget the tea bags,' Frank winked at me and grinned.

Then he turned the key and the engine of our ten-year-old Audi A6 Allroad roared into life. He backed down the driveway and we set off on the road, windows open and Bruce Springsteen blasting from the stereo at full volume.

The Day the Music Died

We were an hour from home, cruising at a steady speed along the M4, when the CD player started to malfunction. First there was a grinding sound. Then the track started to jump, just as Freddie Mercury was singing at full volume about wanting to break free. Then nothing. Frank signalled left and swerved into Membury services.

'What are you doing?' I looked at my watch.

'I'm not driving all the way to Dover with no music,' he said.

I groaned. Our car has a stereo that takes six CDs in a cartridge, which is great because it means you get to listen to hours of music without having to change a CD. Unfortunately, the six-CD stereo is located in the boot. The same boot that was currently crammed full with all our gear.

Frank pulled into a parking space in the service station car park and turned off the engine. I jumped out and walked to the back of the car. I opened the boot and stood in silent contemplation. Frank came to stand beside me.

'Do I have to?' I said.

'Yes,' Frank said. His tone brooked no argument.

'Mum!' The cry came from the backseat. 'Can we go to the loo?'

'Yes,' I said. 'But your father can bloody well take you.'

Twenty minutes later the kids had been to the loo, there was a pile of suitcases on the tarmac behind our car and Frank was wrestling with the stereo, trying to pull out the CD cartridge, but to no avail.

'Daddy?' a cry came from inside the car. 'Are we going to miss our boat?'

Frank ignored the question and turned to me. 'This cartridge just isn't going to come out. Not without me breaking the stereo. I'll have to go to a garage once we get to Europe.'

'Great. So still no music and I've got to repack the boot.'

'Luckily, though,' Frank said with the kind of smile he uses when he has done something clever, 'I brought my old iPod and a mini speaker with me for when we're in the accommodation. It's got our entire early CD collection on it – the music of the 1960s, 1970s, 1980s and 1990s. It'll be like listening to the greatest hits of our youth.'

Frank fished in a suitcase, got out his tech and headed back to the car to set up the temporary music system. I looked in dismay at the pile of suitcases. Then I smiled. What the hell, I thought. Let's get this party started. I pushed up my sleeves and began to shove our belongings back into the boot.

Highway to Hell

We were on the southbound section of the M25 when I started to worry that Frank might be playing his favourite game: petrol roulette. I peered over Frank's shoulder to look at the fuel gauge. I tried to do it so he wouldn't notice. Frank flinched. Damn. I had been spotted.

'Are we going to run out of petrol?' I smiled at him.

'We'll be fine.' Strangely, Frank appeared to have taken my innocent question as an accusation.

We drove another few miles. The petrol needle kept dropping.

'Frank, we won't be fine. We're going to run out of petrol. We're going to miss our ferry. Why do you always have to do this?'

'Because petrol is much cheaper in France. I have a spreadsheet about this. I can show it to you sometime if you like.'

'No, Frank, I don't want to see your damn spreadsheet,' I said.

'Language, mummy!' Edith piped up. (Our family is like an episode of *Absolutely Fabulous* where Frank and I play the roles of Patsy and Edina, and the kids are both Saffy.)

I turned around to address her. 'When we run out of petrol, I reserve the right to say to your father, "I told you so".'

'You can reserve the right to say whatever you like,' Frank said, 'because we're not going to run out of petrol.'

Alfie looked up from his games console. 'Stop it, you two.'

As we rolled down the hill into Dover, Frank was coasting in neutral. The petrol light had come on fifty miles earlier – the petrol light that indicated when the car had fifty miles of petrol left in the tank. We eased over the Dover roundabouts on fumes and drifted to a stop at the ticket booth for the ferry. The attendant checked our tickets and waved us through. We cleared passport control and customs, inching along with the engine idling in neutral. Finally, we arrived at lane 52 and pulled to a stop.

Frank turned off the engine and twisted round in his seat. He smiled at the kids. 'See, I told you we'd make it,' he said.

'We're not in France yet,' I said. 'I'm not sure you should have turned off the engine.'

'All we have to do is drive onto the boat.'

'And drive off it again. And get to a petrol station at the other end.'

'We'll be fine. You worry too much.'

Edith looked up from her games console. 'Stop it, you two.'

'Look, this boat has got sockets!' Alfie could barely contain his excitement. 'Have you got an adaptor so I can charge my DS?'

It was a French boat with French plugs. The adaptors were buried somewhere deep inside the boot.

'I am *not* opening that boot again until we arrive in Amsterdam.' I had just about had enough of my family already, and I had six months more to go. I took some deep breaths.

'No need to get stressed, mum,' Alfie said.

Lorries and cars whizzed past us. We were parked up on the hard shoulder of the E40, which was supposed to be taking us north-east out of Calais towards Belgium. The car rocked from side to side as another giant truck sped by. The hard shoulder was littered with bits of ruptured tyres. But it wasn't our tyres that were the problem. I grimaced at Frank.

'I told you so. I *knew* we'd run out of bloody petrol.'

'And I knew you'd bloody well say that. So now we're even.'

'Stop it, you two,' the kids said in unison.

'And will you *please* stop using so much bad language, mummy,' Edith said.

Frank got out of the car, heaved a sigh and started to make his way down the hard shoulder in the direction of the nearest petrol station. I watched him disappear into the distance. He had learned an important lesson that day. If you play petrol roulette enough times, eventually you will lose.

English Lessons

1   Packing a car for a road trip is an art form. Nominate one chief packer and, once you've given her the job, don't mess with her or her packing.

2   When you go on a road trip take the things you love, especially if they're going to be difficult to get hold of while you're away. We took tea bags, super-sized mugs, decent pillows (one each), children's cuddlies, lots of books and music. Frank packed two extra-large CD wallets for our journey, containing more than 600 CDs in total. But we never did get the CD player to work again after Membury services.

3   It's exciting leaving the country where you live, especially if you live on an island. As we watched the White Cliffs of Dover recede into the distance, it felt like we were breaking free and setting off on an amazing adventure.

4   I don't care what anyone says about screens: Kids + Technology = Stress-Free Travel. That is, until you accidentally blow up the car's cigarette lighter.

5   Learning doesn't only happen in school. Not all holidays are bad; not all absence from school is damaging. Our kids were about to spend six months where they wouldn't sit down and do any formal lessons, but that didn't mean they would stop learning.

6   Freedom of movement around Europe is a wonderful thing. If leaving the EU means that we lose the opportunity to easily travel, live and work elsewhere in Europe, it is the daftest thing my fellow country people have ever voted to do.

7   The euro is also wonderful, especially when combined with free movement. If not for the euro, we would have had to take Dutch guilders, German Deutschemarks, Austrian schillings, Italian lira, Portuguese escudos and French francs with us.

8   Being 'culturally literate' doesn't have to mean only being literate in your own culture.

9   It is quite possible to retain a sense of your own nationality, and to enjoy your own culture, while still celebrating other people's. (Unless your name is Nigel Farage.)

10 There's no need to be afraid of foreigners, and there's no need to be afraid of being a foreigner, either.

Stepping Out of the System

As a parent in the UK, you must make sure that your child has a full time education, once they are of compulsory school age. However, this education does not have to take place in a school. If your personal situation allows, and if you and your children want something different, you can step out of the system altogether. You might do this for a short while, like we did, or as an ongoing commitment to a different way of life. There are all sorts of reasons why people decide to step out of the education system. Some parents do it for philosophical reasons or as a lifestyle choice – they want to spend more time with their children, learning together. Others keep their children out of the system because of dissatisfaction with what they are being offered. Some are making a stand against what they see as excessive government testing. But with an increasing number of jobs no longer tied to a specific location, or to a 9 to 5 working day, home education is becoming a viable option for more and more people. There has been a 65% increase in the number of parents choosing to home educate (or 'unschooling') in the UK over the last six years.

Of course, it's not that simple. If you are going to educate your child at home, or on the road, you will need to ask yourself some important questions:

- How long is it practicable for me to educate my children away from school?
- What about my job? Finances? Partner? Family? House?
- Will it be disruptive to my children, and their school, if I can only home educate them for a short time? Am I being fair?
- Do I want to travel with my children, educate them at home, or a mix of both?
- What do my children think about this? Are they happy with the idea of being educated outside of school, and how would they like to approach it?
- Am I going to do this long term? Do I have access to the right networks and support?

If you decide to home educate your children, you need to remove them from the school roll, by notifying the school. You can apply for a school place again when (or if) you are ready to return. You should note that the school does not have to keep a place open for your child and there is no guarantee that there will be a place for your child in the same school later on. However, your local authority has a duty to ensure that your child has a school place if you request one. If you are only going to home educate your child for a short period of time, some ideal times to do it are when you are:

- Moving from one area to another.
- Returning to the UK from overseas.
- Changing between state and private education, or vice versa.
- Moving from a primary to a secondary school.

In these situations, you will be taking your child off roll at one school and registering them at another one anyway. You can simply remove them from school a bit earlier than you would have done and fill in the gap yourself. In England, you must apply for a secondary school place by 31 October, and you will be told which place you have been allocated on 1 March the following year. This means that there is a period in the last year of primary school when you can remove your child from the primary school and still retain their place at secondary school. (And, handily, if this is your goal, avoid Year 6 national tests.) If you choose this option, when you contact your local authority to take your child off the roll, let them know that you still want your child's secondary school place.

You can also ask your child's school and your local authority whether they would be willing for your child to be educated partly at school and partly at home. This option is known as 'flexi-schooling' and it is sometimes used when a child struggles to attend school full time — for instance, if they have an ongoing illness. However, the school and the local authority do not have to agree to this option. If you decide to put your child back into the school system after a break, share stories of what you did while you were away and let the teachers know how it has benefited your child.

If you are considering home education:

- The websites www.home-education.org.uk, www.edyourself.org and www.educationotherwise.net offer a very useful starting point. Tap into the various local networks of support.
- For parents in Scotland, the charity www.schoolhouse.org.uk gives helpful advice.

- If your child has a special educational need or disability, you must take this into account in the educational provision you offer.
- In England, your local authority can make an 'informal enquiry' to see whether you are providing a suitable education, but their rights to inspect what you do are fairly limited.

The situation regarding home education varies according to where you live, and you may wish to take independent legal advice to clarify your position. The following links give a basic overview of the legal position:

- If you are based in England, see: www.gov.uk/school-attendance-absence/overview and www.gov.uk/home-education.
- For Scotland, see: www.educationscotland.gov.uk/parentzone/myschool/choosingaschool/homeeducation/index.asp.
- For Wales, see: www.waleshomeeducation.co.uk/the-law.php.
- For Northern Ireland, see: www.nidirect.gov.uk/articles/educating-your-child-home. NB: compulsory school age in Northern Ireland is from 4 years old.

In the afternoon we saw where Anne Frank hid for two years. The rooms where they stayed were very small and they couldn't make any sounds or open the curtains during the day. They were found in 1944 and taken to a concentration camp. Anne died there a month before liberation.

My favourite guns were the swan guns which shot a hail of bullets that would kill an entire flock of swans; also having a 3 metre long barrel. There was another cool early machine gun which was multibarreled and operated by one hand. Most of the early guns where made for specific needs and took a while to reload.

The Netherlands

Van Gogh

At the Van Gogh museum we learnt about Van and his paintings. Van Gogh was an artist for 10 years but his paintings are some of the best in the world. At first his paintings we dark and gloomy but over time they got brighter and more colourful. He used many different painting techniques including dots, dashes, swirls and urls.

Today we played in the park and climbed on the letters of I AMSTERDAM. After that we had our picnic. Then we walked to the Rijks Museum. There was almost everything on humans. In the Rijks museum there were weapons, jewlry, clothes, pottery and models of ships. We also saw medals, coins, statues and doll houses. We didn't see all of the museum but it was very interesting.

Our House

As we pulled into the campsite on the outskirts of Amsterdam, there were bunnies hopping around in the twilight. This delighted the kids. I think Frank saw the bunnies as a potential source of dinner, though, given the speed at which he drove through the campsite. It had taken me a lot of time and an awful lot of Internet research to decide where we should stay in Amsterdam. I was hoping that I had struck gold with the first booking of our tour.

'You cannot be serious,' Frank pulled up to the mobile home and turned off the engine. He turned to me with a troubled look on his face. 'You booked this? You expect us to stay here?'

'What's wrong with it?'

'What's right with it, you mean.' Frank opened his door and got out.

'I spent a lot of time on Google,' I said, getting out of the car too. 'I found out all about accommodation in Amsterdam. And I'm telling you, Frank, this was the best option I could find. It was either this campsite or a pricey hotel in town with no parking, tiny bedrooms, a shared toilet, lots of stairs, no lifts and crack addicts in the hallways. Don't shoot the accommodation booker.' Frank raised an eyebrow but wisely kept his mouth shut.

We got out of the car and everyone stretched their backs and shook out their legs. It had been a long journey across England, into France, through Belgium and finally to the Netherlands. What I was now referring to as 'that bloody petrol incident' had cost us an hour. We were tired, hungry and ready to collapse into a large comfy bed. Unfortunately, it appeared that we were not going to be spending the next few nights in a large comfy bed. As he entered the mobile home, Frank ducked his head to look into the bedroom. He had to duck his head because the doorways were so low.

'I'm six foot five,' Frank said. 'I can't sleep in that bed. It's only five feet long.'

We squeezed though a narrow gangway that ran down one side

of the mobile home, alongside the bedrooms. On the other side of the passage was a sink, a fridge and a couple of gas hobs.

'How am I supposed to cook in a kitchen where two people can't even pass each other sideways?' Frank said.

'I'll do the cooking,' I forced a smile. 'And the kids can do the washing up.' Alfie and Edith exchanged an incredulous look. 'This is a lovely big sitting area, isn't it?' I moved into the main part of the mobile home and swept my hand around it to indicate the spacious accommodation, like I was Kirstie Allsopp on a European edition of *Location, Location, Location*. Soon I would be suggesting that we knock down a wall or two and remodel the interior.

'Mum!' Edith called from the bedroom. She sounded horrified. I hurried back to see what was wrong.

'Why are there no windows in our bedroom?' Edith said.

'And why does it smell of poo?' Alfie held his nose.

'Well, even if you all hate my choice of accommodation, luckily it's a safe and easy five minute walk to the nearest metro station,' I said. 'At least that's what it said when I checked it on Google.'

The next morning we would discover that the nearest station was half an hour's walk away, across a six-lane highway.

Art for Art's Sake

After a cramped and restless night's sleep, and a long and danger-ous walk to the metro station, we had finally made it into the centre of Amsterdam. The kids were clambering all over the massive letters of the 'I Amsterdam' sign, next to the Rijksmuseum. Edith was balancing precariously on top of the 'e'. Alfie was sliding down the 'a'. It was lucky we didn't call them Felicity and Zack or they would have felt seriously disadvantaged by that sign.

'Hey kids!' I said. 'Have you finished climbing yet? Can we go to the Van Gogh Museum now?'

'Leave them alone,' Frank yawned. 'They're having fun.'

'This is Road School. We're not meant to be having fun. We're meant to be doing educational things.'

'Think of it as PE,' Frank yawned again. 'And, anyway, they need to stretch their legs after spending the night in a tiny tin box.'

Edith waved at me and shouted, 'Take a photo of me on the "e", mum!'

Alfie yelled over to us as well, 'And one of me on the "a"!'

'Van Gogh painted more than 2,000 paintings, but he only sold one during his lifetime.' I was reading from *The Rough Guide to Amsterdam* as we made our way across the Museumsplein towards the Van Gogh Museum.

'Poor guy,' Edith said. 'He must have been gutted about that.'

'Maybe he should have got the message that nobody liked his paintings sometime before his two thousandth picture,' Alfie said.

'Ah, but he didn't make art for money's sake, he made art for art's sake,' I replied.

'Well, that's just dumb,' Alfie said.

'Yes, but now his paintings sell for millions of pounds,' Edith said.

'That's not much good to Van Gogh, though, is it?' Frank pointed out. 'Given that he's dead.'

'Edith? Alfie? Which of Van Gogh's paintings do you like best?' We were wandering around the upper floor of the museum. The paintings were displayed in the order in which they had been painted. Van Gogh's early paintings were dark and lifelike. His later and more famous pictures were full of colour and far more abstract.

'I like this one,' Alfie was staring in fascination at one of Van Gogh's early works. 'It's really dark and it's got a skull in it. It looks evil.'

'I like this one,' Edith was on the other side of the open space.

She was examining one of the later paintings. 'The flowers are very beautiful colours. It looks so pretty.' (Our kids certainly knew how to buck male and female stereotypes.)

'Do you think you'd like to be an artist when you grow up?' I walked over to where Edith was standing. She had mentioned this as a possibility in the past. I was keen to explore the idea with her on our trip by taking the kids to as many art galleries as we could.

'Yes!' she said. 'I'd love to be an artist!'

I was delighted to hear this. 'And why do you want to be an artist so much?' I felt sure in my heart that she would say something deep and meaningful about how it would allow her to express herself or how it would give her life value.

'Because if I become an artist I can be famous and make lots of money,' Edith said, with a massive grin on her face.

Tears Are Not Enough

It was easy to tell where the Anne Frank House was because of the long queue of tourists snaking down the street outside the building. There was a cold wind blowing through the narrow lanes of Amsterdam, and there was a hint of rain in the air. A set of barriers indicated the area where people could wait to enter the house.

'There's a queue,' Frank said. 'Why is there always a queue?'

'It won't take long,' I said. 'And, anyway, queuing is a British value. Which means it's educational. Plus, we're naturally good at queuing, given that we're British.'

'Sod British values. I don't do queues. I'm going for a coffee.' Frank pointed to a cafe on the other side of the canal. 'I'll be over there where it's warm and there's hot coffee and free Wi-Fi.'

'Can we come with you?' The kids said it a touch too eagerly for my liking.

'No, you can't!' I glared at them, daring them to argue.

Frank headed off over the canal bridge. We shuffled forwards in the queue, shivering in the cold. It was less than five minutes before the kids started complaining.

'I'm bored,' said Alfie.

'So am I,' said Edith.

'Are you sure we can't just go and join dad?' Alfie looked longingly across the canal at the steamed up windows of the cafe. It looked warm, comfy and inviting in there.

'No, you can't!'

'I need the loo.' Edith started jiggling her legs in the internationally recognisable 'I am a child who needs a wee' signal. 'There's probably a toilet in that cafe where dad went to wait.'

'You'll just have to wait until we get inside.' Heavy drops of rain began to plop down on us from the darkening sky.

'I'm cold.' Alfie hugged his arms tight around his body.

'I'm getting wet.' Edith pulled up her hood as the rain began to fall more quickly, and jiggled even more furiously than before.

'Are you sure we can't …?' Alfie began.

'No! You are *not* going to the cafe!'

'There's no need to get all shouty and stressed, mum,' Alfie said.

I bought our tickets while Edith dashed off to use the toilets, then we went through a barrier and into the main part of the building. The moment we stepped into Anne's house, the tears started to fall down my face.

'Are you okay, mum?' Alfie looked concerned.

'I'm fine.' I swiped away the tears with the back of my hand and sniffed loudly.

'You don't look fine,' Alfie said.

'Are you sure you're okay, mum?' Edith said.

'Really, I'm fine. It's just very sad.'

'What is?' Alfie said. We hadn't even got to the point in the Anne Frank House where the story unfolds, so I didn't know how to answer his question.

The tears kept streaming down my face. Before long I stopped trying to wipe them away because they just kept coming. I could barely see where I was going. Snot began to drip off the end of my nose. I pushed the kids ahead of me and followed on behind them, so that they wouldn't have to see my red cheeks and my bleary eyes.

The atmosphere inside the house felt frozen in time: it had been left untouched, like a time capsule taking us back to the desperate days of the Second World War. We trudged slowly up the narrow stairs, the walls pressing in on all sides. The air felt thick and heavy, as though a cloud had descended upon us. A quiet had come over the crowd of tourists. They inched along the narrow corridors. People were muttering among themselves in whispered tones. It was hard to think of anything even remotely appropriate to say in this place.

Eventually we arrived at the bookcase that concealed the entrance to the secret annexe. It was the kind of bookcase that features in children's dreams, where a magical world is hidden behind a secret door. Except that this bookcase didn't lead to the world of the imagination, it led to a place of fear and death. We stepped through the entrance into a series of darkened, silent hiding spaces: the rooms where Anne Frank, her family and friends hid from the Nazis. All around us, people fell completely silent.

The most heart-breaking thing in the hidden rooms was a height chart, drawn by Anne on her bedroom wall. The marks are preserved behind a Perspex screen. I reached up to touch the plastic with tears still dripping down my face. The lines reminded me of the height marks that our children had scratched on their own bedroom walls to denote the passage of time. These marks were so normal, so unexpected and so childlike. They told the story of Anne's years of captivity in this claustrophobic place far more eloquently than any words could ever have done.

Even though I knew how the story ended, I found myself hoping that the outcome would be different. That we wouldn't learn how Anne was eventually discovered, captured by the Nazis and how she died in Bergen-Belsen just before liberation. That our children wouldn't have to learn the truth about how cruel people can be to their fellow human beings. We left the secret rooms and came out into the final display, where we found out how this story ended and how there was no happily ever after for little Anne Frank.

Then, a bit shell-shocked by the experience, we left the Anne Frank House, crossed the bridge over the canal and went to join Frank in the Internet cafe.

'I think I might have overdone it on the coffee.' Frank was typing numbers into a spreadsheet and his hands were shaking with caffeine overload. 'Did you have a good time?'

'Me and Alfie did,' Edith said, 'but I don't think mummy did. She cried the whole way round.'

Weeks later, when we were walking through the ruins of Pompeii, Alfie said something that brought me skidding back to those moments in the Anne Frank House, and to the tears that kept sliding down my face.

'I think I know why you're not crying here in Pompeii, mum, like you did when we were at the Anne Frank House. Even though lots of people died in Pompeii too.'

'Why's that?' To be honest, I wasn't really sure myself.

'Because what happened here at Pompeii was a natural phenomenon,' he said. 'But people murdered Anne Frank. And they didn't have to do that. They could have said no.'

A few months after our trip finished, when the kids were back in school, Edith came home one day and announced that her new class topic was the Second World War. That night she took Anne Frank's diary from her bookshelf. I had bought it for her before Road School began and taken it with us on our trip, but she had not read it at the time. That evening she snuggled up next to me on the sofa and worked her way through Anne's diary. As she turned the final few pages, tears began to pour down her face. Her small body was racked with sobs. She was inconsolable with grief for Anne.

Before we set off on our Road School trip, I wasn't sure that you could teach empathy. I still don't think you can, at least not in the traditional sense of teaching something. But you can learn it. And maybe being there, going to Anne's house and visiting the ruins of Pompeii, had helped our kids to understand just a little bit more what empathy really means.

Absolute Beginners

'Be careful as you get off the tram,' I said. 'Make sure you watch out for cars. And for trams. And for bikes. Especially bikes. There are lots and lots of bikes in Amsterdam.'

'Okay,' the kids said, hanging on to the rail for dear life as the tram pulled to a violent stop.

'Leave them alone,' Frank said. 'Stop mollycoddling them. They'll be fine. They have brains in their heads and eyes in their faces.'

'They need to know this stuff,' I said. 'This kind of knowledge is very important when you've only just arrived somewhere.'

We stepped off the tram and onto a narrow strip of pavement that ran between the tramlines and the pavement at the side of the road. Edith looked to the right for traffic. Then she stepped into the road and was almost mown down by a speeding cyclist. The cyclist wobbled precariously and screeched to a halt, barely managing to stay on his bike. He shouted furiously at us in Dutch and then rode off into the distance, shaking his fist.

'Are you okay?' I picked Edith up, dusted her down and checked her over for damage.

'Maybe you should have reminded her that they drive on the other side of the road here,' Frank said. 'That particular bit of knowledge is indispensable when you're in Europe.'

The tram had dropped us at the Museumplein again, for a second day of art and culture. First on the itinerary was the Rijksmuseum, but before we could start our visit Alfie and Edith informed us that it was essential for physical education reasons that they got to climb all over the 'I Amsterdam' sign again. Edith clambered to the top of the 'e', then slid underneath it and settled into a comfy position on the tail. Alfie squished himself through the centre of the 'a' as though it was a tunnel. Frank and I slumped on a nearby bench to warm up in the sunshine. It had been another cramped and uncomfortable night in our too short bed in our too small mobile home. Frank closed his eyes and a few moments later the sound of snoring came from alongside me.

'Wake up,' I tapped him on the arm.

'I wasn't asleep,' Frank said. 'I was just resting my eyes.'

Half an hour later we extracted the kids from the sign before they took up permanent residence on it. We made our way into the Rijksmuseum as so many millions of knowledge seeking tourists had done before us. As we entered the foyer, I could sense the centuries of history and culture echoing around the space. The building was filled with tourists from all over the world, here to commune with the culture of the past. We queued up to buy our tickets and then paused for a moment in the large open foyer, deciding on how best to tackle our tour.

'There's tons of stuff in here,' I consulted the museum guide. 'We won't have time to see everything, so let's narrow it down. What are you really, really, really interested in?' Interest was the acid test for Road School, after all.

'I want to see the arms exhibit,' Alfie said. 'I like weapons.'

'That sounds good,' Frank said, 'and educational too, obviously.' Frank likes weapons as well.

'It sounds more violent than educational to me,' I said.

'I like violence,' Alfie said.

'I want to see if they've got any paintings by Leonardo da Vinci. I love Leonardo so much.' There was a dreamy look in Edith's eyes. She was definitely getting a bit obsessed with this da Vinci guy.

I took charge. 'Let's do weapons first and Leonardo next. Then we'll decide what we want to do after that.'

The arms exhibit was just off the main foyer to the right. We showed our tickets, then we slipped inside. We entered a quiet space full of gleaming pistols in sparkling glass cases and silvery suits of armour shining under the spotlights.

'*Look at all these guns!*' Alfie's jaw dropped open in wonder. It was pretty impressive how quickly our children could destroy the atmosphere of a peaceful and civilised museum. The tourists who had been quietly studying the exhibits until we arrived all looked in our direction. The attendant made a kind of embarrassed shushing sound. Alfie was oblivious. He leaned his palms against the glass of the first display case and began to drool. He shifted along the glass case, staring intently at each of the guns and leaving smeared fingerprints behind him.

'Look dad, it's a swan gun!' Alfie said. 'It shoots a hail of bullets that can kill an entire flock of swans. And it has a three metre long barrel!'

He sprinted towards the next exhibit. 'Look! It's an early machine gun. It was multi-barrelled and operated by one hand!'

It only took a few steps for him to reach an even larger weapon. 'Look! It's a cannon!' Clearly our son still had quite a bit of learning to do on the empathy front.

Edith was more taken with the shining suit of armour. 'How did they move around in that?' she wanted to know. 'Hey, take a photo of me next to it, mum!' The camera flashed as I took the photo, a burst of light reflecting off the glass case and the armour inside. The attendant scurried over to us with a scowl on her face, said something in Dutch and pointed at the 'no camera flash' sign stuck to the glass cabinet.

'Where to next?' We staggered dazed out of the darkness of the arms display and back into the bright central foyer. After our initial behaviour the attendant had trailed around after us for the entire time we were inside. I could swear I heard her breathe a sigh of relief when we finally exited.

'It's my turn now,' Edith grabbed the museum map from me and flicked through it. 'I want to see if they've got anything by Leonardo, then we should do jewellery, pottery, models of ships and dolls houses.'

'And then can we do medals and coins?' Alfie said.

'Sure thing,' I said. 'But could we maybe keep it down a bit in the next section?' With this much knowledge on offer it was going to be a very fruitful visit. That was, unless we became the first family ever to get banned from the Rijksmuseum for bad behaviour.

Smoke On the Water

'I am *not* going on a canal boat,' Frank said as we trudged back towards the train station, exhausted after a day of rampant tourism. 'I've been on that canal trip more times than I can count. The canals stink. And the boats drift along so slowly it drives you mad. I'll go back to the mobile home and organise dinner.'

'You mean "have a snooze",' I said.

'As if I'd do such a thing. Anyway, I'll see you all in a couple of hours.' Frank headed off in the direction of the station before I could protest any further.

The canal boat did indeed drift very slowly between the rows of houseboats. The canal was stinky, just as Frank had predicted. A misty drizzle hung above the water as we passed under endless low bridges. The running commentary told us all kinds of facts about the canals and the buildings that lined them. We gazed out of the window of the boat, at the homes along the banks.

'I would so love to live on a houseboat one day,' Edith sighed.

'You could do that,' I said. 'No reason why not. The world is your oyster. At least Europe is. So long as the UK doesn't vote to leave the EU.'

'What's the EU?' she said. 'And why is the UK going to vote to leave it?'

'It's a long story. Probably best to ask your father.'

'This canal is smelly,' Alfie said. 'I don't think I'd like to live here.'

'Well, you don't have to,' his sister said, 'but I might.'

We sat in silence for a bit, listening to the commentary and watching the world pass by. Down here on the canal we were below street level, in a world of water and low bridges. It felt as though there were two Amsterdams – the bustling noisy streets full of trams and bicycles, where you were in danger of being mown down at any moment, and the slow, quiet but smelly solitude of the canals.

'Mum,' Edith said. 'Why do the houses look so different here?'

'Well, the architecture is different in different parts of Europe. That's something you'll notice as we travel around.'

'Are the Dutch people really tall and thin? Their houses are very tall and skinny.'

'And aren't the houses kind of leaning over?' Alfie joined in our architectural discussion. It was starting to feel like I was in an episode of *Grand Designs*.

'The houses are narrow because when they were built the people got taxed on the width of their frontage,' I read from the guidebook. 'So obviously they made their houses as narrow as they could. And this meant that they had really thin staircases too. Do you see the hooks at the top of the houses?' The children nodded. 'Well, they use those to pull goods and furniture up to the top of their houses because the stairs are too narrow to get anything up there. And the houses had to lean forwards so that the furniture didn't hit the building on the way up.'

'Hello?' I called, opening the door to the mobile home and dragging myself inside. The kids limped their way in behind me. We were exhausted. This tourism thing was hard work, and it was a very long walk from the station back to the campsite. There was no reply. There was also no sight, sound or smell of dinner.

'Hello?' I called a bit louder. A loud snore erupted from the sofa. Frank was 'resting his eyes' again.

'I was right about the snooze then,' I said.

'Daddy, daddy!' Edith rushed over and jumped on her father. Frank sat up and tried to look like he hadn't been napping.

'Yes, darling, what is it? Did you have a lovely time on the canal boat?'

'What's the EU, and why might we leave it?' she said. 'Mum says I won't be able to live on a canal boat when I'm older because people might vote to leave the EU.'

Frank laughed. 'What on earth has your mum been telling you?

Of course we're not going to vote to leave the EU. No one could be that stupid. Not even the British.'

Dutch Lessons

1 Don't overestimate the British.

2 Don't believe everything you read on Google. Don't be too optimistic about the information you get from TripAdvisor either.

3 Size matters. A six foot five inch man does not fit into a five foot nothing bed. Frank would remind me frequently about his height over the coming months as we experienced the cramped budget accommodation of Europe and China.

4 While it's important to gain knowledge, often the best knowledge comes through experience. It is perfectly possible for you to be taught something that is wrong or for you to misinterpret what you heard (as I found out to my cost when I was booking accommodation). All the knowledge in the world is not much help unless you have the ability to evaluate it.

5 You can learn about art in books. You can look at images of art on the Internet. But there is nothing like seeing original works of art in real life. As schools are forced to make more and more time for subjects that are tested, art is in danger of being squeezed out of the curriculum.

6 You can figure out a lot about a country and its people by looking at their architecture and their public art. The 'I Amsterdam' sign is a perfect metaphor for the Dutch attitude to life. You can play, climb or chill out on it, according to your needs.

7 A city full of bikes is great for the environment, but if you're not careful it can be extremely injurious to your health.

8 History comes to life through the stories of the people who lived it. Children can relate to the tragic story of a young girl like Anne Frank because they can imagine themselves in her position.

9 History also comes to life through the objects of the past. Seeing real-life artefacts, even if only behind glass cases in a museum, helps children to gain a multi-sensory view of the past.

10 You can't necessarily test the things that matter. You can't test joy, or love, or happiness, or pleasure. Maybe the best test of what our kids learned on our journey would be to ask them what they remember about it in forty years' time. Or if they decide to go travelling with their families when they are older.

The Practicalities

The idea of going on the road with your children for six months or more sounds very exciting and romantic, but it's not all sweetness and light. As we very quickly found out, there are the day-to-day realities of travelling to contend with. Any road trip costs money, and if you are away from home it can be tricky to earn it. You will either need to save up ahead of time or find a way to make travelling pay. There are opportunities for work overseas, or if you have a job that can be done online (like writing) you can work from anywhere in the world. If you are travelling as a couple, one of you might do freelance work while the other person educates the children. If you're in permanent employment, you could try asking your employer about taking a sabbatical. Remember that the costs of travel are lower when you are home educating because you can travel off-season and out of the school holiday periods.

When you plan the timing of your trip:

- Watch out for unexpected public holidays – these will be different in every country you visit.
- Consider what the weather will be like in the countries you go to and how this might affect your comfort when visiting tourist sites.
- Check for any special events that might make a location busier than usual.
- Find out about any planned road closures or industrial action that might affect your journey.
- Factor in enough time to have any vaccinations you might need and to apply for visas.

There are various ways to help make a trip more affordable, either by earning money while you are away or saving money as you go.

Before you go:

- If you own a flat or house, you could rent this out short term while you are away, or sell up if you don't plan on coming back.
- When you book accommodation, buy tickets, insurance, etc. for your trip, do it via a cashback site and you can receive 10% or more back. We used www.topcashback.co.uk.

- When you book accommodation, check several hotel booking websites to find out what is available in different countries, as some sites have better coverage than others.
- Think laterally about your options. If you're not a fan of camping, many campsites also have mobile homes available.
- Work out a budget and identify places where you can make savings – for instance, staying longer in locations where accommodation is cheaper.
- Sign up for an account with the various accommodation websites – this makes managing your bookings easier, and some sites offer incentives when you make a number of bookings. We used a combination of www.hotels.com, www.booking.com and www.ownersdirect.co.uk depending on the type of accommodation we wanted and the availability for the country we were in.
- If you've got family or friends overseas, ask if you can stay with them for a while.
- Do some research to find out which items are going to be more expensive to buy while you are away. For instance, batteries are much more expensive in some countries than in others.
- Buy your currency in as large an amount as you can, so that you get the best exchange rate.
- Your normal credit card may charge you a fee for using it abroad, plus a fee for the foreign exchange, and also give you a poor exchange rate. Some credit card companies do not charge fees for overseas transactions – for instance, the Post Office.
- Norwich & Peterborough Building Society have a current account where you can withdraw money from ATMs anywhere in the world without paying fees or currency exchange charges.

For detailed advice and all the latest ideas for making savings on travel, visit Martin Lewis's www.moneysavingexpert.com website.

While you're away

- You could write a blog about your travels linked to products or services. Some bloggers receive free products in return for writing about them. Others host advertising on their sites. For a list of the top 50 travel blogs see: www.theexpeditioner.com/the-top-50-travel-blogs/.
- At each location you visit, look into all-inclusive deals, such as city

cards for money off when visiting attractions or transport cards that you can use on different forms of public transport.

- Consider staying outside the major cities and using public transport to travel in, as accommodation charges can be much lower in the suburbs.
- Plan ahead when purchasing fuel – the savings mount up if you are doing thousands of miles. Service stations typically add a large mark-up to fuel prices; a short detour off the motorway can save you a significant amount of money.
- Book self-catering accommodation, even if this costs slightly more than other options, because the savings from making your own meals will far outweigh the difference.
- Remember that it can be very pricey to buy snacks and drinks and to eat out during the day, especially in capital cities. You can save yourself a considerable amount of money by making packed lunches and taking your own drinks with you.
- Keep an eye out for free events and for days or times when you can get free entry to galleries, museums, etc. At many of the places we visited, children paid half the price or got free entry.

It is very important indeed to take out a decent travel insurance policy, especially if you are going to be travelling outside the European Union. Make sure that you have an up to date European Health Insurance Card (EHIC) for each member of your family, so that you have access to free medical treatment within the EU. If you pay any medical charges, keep your receipts and you should be able to claim these back on your return.

Transport

Your choice of transport will depend on how far you are going and your family's personal preferences. For long distance destinations, flights are the most realistic option. The website www.momondo.co.uk allows you to check the cheapest times, dates and days to fly to different parts of the world. If you are planning to visit destinations closer to home, think about what the cheapest form of transport will be at each point in your trip. Although you might imagine that train travel would be cheaper than car travel, with a family of four, driving may be less expensive. Take into account all the hidden costs – for instance, the cost of driving includes road tolls and repairs on your vehicle, as well as fuel. If you are travelling long distances within Europe, consider taking your car on a boat. There are routes from the UK to Spain and to various destinations in the Mediterranean. Taking a boat is a lot more relaxing than driving and there are some bargains to be had out of season.

When we first decided to go on our trip, I had the idea that it would be lovely to buy a camper van and to travel around Europe in a 'home' of our own. On the plus side, nightly accommodation charges are cheaper with a camper van than booking a hotel room or hiring an apartment. You also have all your own things with you and there is no need to unpack them into a separate space each time you move on. On the down side, it is tricky to drive a camper van into the middle of a major city, and ferry tickets, tolls and fuel are all more costly when you travel in a large vehicle. The cost of hiring a camper van, even long term, turned out to be more than the cost of booking hotels or apartments. Plus, living in one space as a family for a long time wouldn't have been great for our personal life either. In the end, I came to the conclusion that, for our family at least, Frank was correct to reject my suggestion.

Packing

Packing ends up becoming an art form when you are spending a long time away from home. Remember that, whatever you might need on your travels, you will probably be able to buy most of it where you are going (especially in Europe). If you're in a vehicle, work out what needs to be accessible and what can be tucked away. It's helpful if you don't need to unpack all your long-term supplies every time you book into new accommodation.

- Allocate a couple of suitcases to contain a full set of everything you need for a short stay. I had one bag with a change of clothes and toiletries for everyone, and a second bag with my kitchen equipment.
- Give your children at least one bag of their own, and encourage them to take responsibility for deciding what to pack in it.
- Look into the different kinds of weather you are likely to experience and pack accordingly. During our tour of Europe, we went from hats and gloves in the snow to swimsuits and towels on the beach.
- Pack those items that are essential for cooking, but that you don't want to have to buy in large quantities, such as salt, pepper and olive oil. Sachets of condiments such as sugar and ketchup are easier to transport than bottles or bags.

- ⛵ A pack of disposable cutlery comes in very handy.
- ⛵ Take a first aid kit and a full supply of any medicines. Work out how you are going to get medications if you need them while you are away by talking to your doctor about your options. Some prescription medicines are available over the counter in parts of Europe.
- ⛵ Include hand washing powder for the times when you don't have access to a washing machine. Pegs are very useful as well.
- ⛵ Take some tin foil, cling film and a set of Tupperware for all those cut-price packed lunches you are going to be making.
- ⛵ Pack a couple of rucksacks to take with you when you are out and about.
- ⛵ Bring a torch and spare batteries.

If you are travelling on from a location, but returning to the same place at a later date, find out whether you can leave some luggage in a storage room at your hotel or in a locker in a nearby railway station or airport. For instance, when we travelled to Xi'an and Shanghai by train, we took a slimmed down set of luggage with us and picked up the rest of our bags on our return. Factor in opportunities to wash your clothes. We took enough to keep us going for about ten days, and I booked an apartment with a washing machine at regular intervals. It is also worth thinking about how you will find space to bring back souvenirs – you could take a spare bag or dispose of items you no longer need along the way.

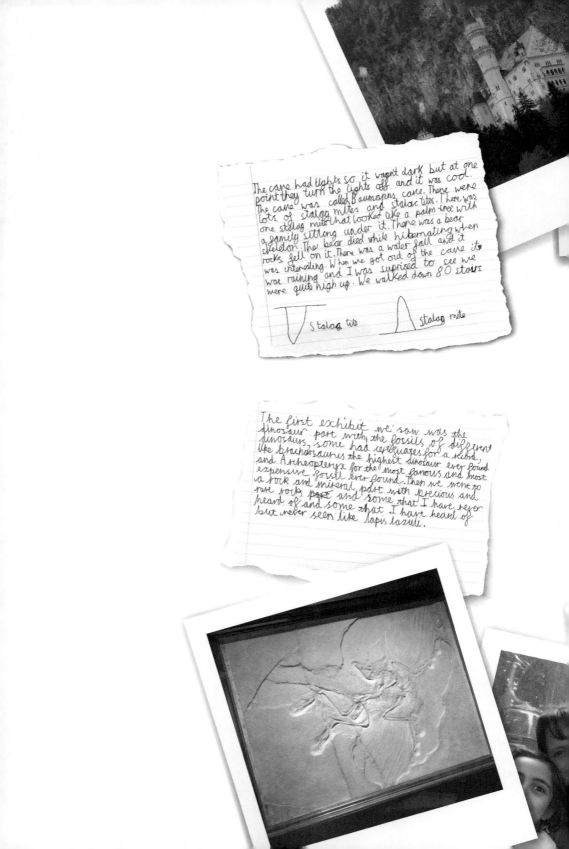

The cave had lights so it wasn't dark but at one point they turn the lights off and it was cool. The cave was called Baumanns cave. There were lots of stalagmites and stalactites. There was one stalagmite that looked like a palm tree with a family sitting under it. There was a bear skeleton. The bear died while hibernating when rocks fell on it. There was a water fall and it was interesting. When we got out of the cave it was raining and I was suprised to see we were quite high up. We walked down 80 stairs

stalagtite   stalagmite

The first exhibit we saw was the dinosaur part with the fossils of different dinosaurs, some had certificates for a record, like brachiosaurus the highest dinosaur ever found and Archeopteryx for the most famous and most expensive fossil ever found. Then we went to a rock and mineral part with precious and rare rocks and some that I have never heard of and some that I have heard of but never seen like lapis lazuli.

The next part of our day was also very interesting, we went to a thermo pool, an incredibly warm heated pool, outside and in. The outside one had a current in it and was very fun. The ones inside where different one was just regular heated pool others where jacuzzis, one was a pool bar. Outside it started snowing which made it even more fun!

Germany

Brandenburg Gate

Today we went to a circus. It was great. There there horses, ponies and a camel. There was a man who did amazing juggling and breathed fire. There were some people who jumped high and did somersaults in mid air. They jumped over horses and a camel; one even did a back flip. We saw 4 ponies 1 of them doing very good tricks. There was a break and we got some candy floss. Then we went back inside.

It's the End of the World As We Know It

It was 1989. We were at a beach cafe in Kovalam, in the state of Kerala, in the far south of India. We were young and slim, and doing the obligatory tour of Southeast Asia. Parenthood was well over a decade away in the future.

'Listen!' There was a note of amazement in Frank's voice. 'Did you hear that?' There was a radio in the corner of the cafe. It was tuned to the BBC World Service.

'No,' I said. 'What is it? What's going on?'

'It's the Berlin Wall. It's been breached. People are climbing onto it. They're crossing into West Germany from the East. Can you believe it?'

We both fell silent for a moment. We were brought up during the Cold War; we had both read 'How to Prepare for a Nuclear War' booklets when we were kids. This was history in the making. It was the fall of the Iron Curtain.

'I'd love to go to Berlin one day,' I said.

Twenty-five years later, we pulled up outside an apartment block in the suburbs of Berlin. We were a lot older, quite a bit fatter and these days we lived our lives with two kids in tow.

'The fifth floor?' Frank jingled the keys to the flat in his hand and looked across at the tall building opposite.

'Err, yes,' I looked up at the apartment block. It was a lot taller than it had looked in the website listing.

'The top floor?' Frank peered upwards.

'Err, yes.'

'I hope there's a lift.'

'Err, no, I don't think there is.' I looked over at the large pile of suitcases that we needed to empty from the car boot, then back up to the top of the building.

'Right, kids,' Frank sighed heavily. 'It's PE time again. Thanks to your mother. But this time round we're doing weight lifting and mountain climbing. Grab a suitcase and follow me.'

After a fifteen minute relay in which I dragged the cases across the road and into the entrance hall, and Frank and the kids lugged the cases up five flights of stairs, we were done. Our bags were all in the apartment, and we could finally settle down for a rest before a few days of exploring Berlin.

'This is a great flat,' I pulled the last of the cases into the large, bright top-floor flat and looked around. There was plenty of space. There was a big bedroom, a comfy looking sofa bed and a good-sized kitchen with a kettle. There was even a terrace outside with a view across the rooftops of Berlin. After the disastrous accommodation in Amsterdam I was chuffed with myself. 'Isn't it great? Don't you agree? Kids? Frank?'

There was a loud groan from the sofa bed. Alfie, Edith and Frank were sprawled on their backs, breathing heavily.

'My legs,' Edith said.

'My arms,' Alfie said.

'My poor aching back,' Frank said.

'Well, there's just no pleasing some people,' I said. 'I'll put the kettle on.'

Another Brick in the Wall

We were in the centre of Berlin, on the Ebertstraße. The road was lined with a row of grey paving slabs marking where the Berlin Wall used to be. A small brass plaque was fixed into one of the slabs, saying 'Berliner Mauer 1969–1989'. The kids were jumping from side to side across the wall that was no longer there.

'I'm in East Germany!' Alfie said.

'I'm in West Germany!' Edith said.

They swapped sides.

'Now I'm in West Germany!' Alfie said.

'And I'm in East Germany!' Edith said.

They had been playing this game for about ten minutes, as Frank told them stories of the Second World War and the Cold War, and why the wall had been built. In my mind I had been drifting back to the time in India, twenty-five years earlier, when we heard that the Iron Curtain had started to fall.

'So that's the story of why the Berlin Wall was erected, and how eventually it fell. And that is the Brandenburg Gate, kids.' Frank pointed behind us to a triumphant looking set of columns with a group of horses on top.

'What? That big grey stone arch thing with the columns on it?' Alfie said. 'What's that for?'

'It was commissioned by Friedrich Wilhelm II as a sign of peace. It was built in the late 1700s. Napoleon used it for a triumphal procession, and the Nazis used it as a symbol of the National Socialist German Workers' Party.'

'How did you know that?' Frank often surprises me with random bits of history. He went to boarding school which might explain his extensive historical knowledge.

'Wikipedia,' he said.

'Ah.' Not boarding school then.

Alfie looked the Brandenburg Gate up and down. 'It's a bit boring.'

His sister gave her assessment: 'It's just a big square lump of grey stone, really, isn't it?'

'Philistines,' Frank muttered under his breath.

'What's a philistine?' Edith wanted to know.

Over by the Brandenburg Gate, I could see a group of tourists clambering on board a large rickshaw on the side of which was an advert for a 'Beer Tour of Berlin'. The rickshaw driver was handing large glasses to the tourists. The glasses were filled to the brim with golden beer. The tourists took their drinks and downed half of the beer in one go. I licked my lips. I suddenly felt very thirsty.

'Those people are philistines,' I pointed over to where the Beer Tour of Berlin was getting ready to depart.

'I think I'd refer to them more as connoisseurs of the golden hop, actually. In fact, that looks like fun. Maybe we could do that tour later on?' Frank looked at me with a hopeful smile on his face.

'What's a connoisseur?' Edith wanted to know.

We went to sit on an area of scrubby grass in front of the

Reichstag to have our picnic. While we ate our sandwiches, Frank regaled us with more of his knowledge of German political history. Frank lived in Germany for several years when he was younger, so he knew a lot about all things German.

'Shall we go and have a look at the Holocaust Memorial?' I packed away the remnants of our lunch.

'Is it more interesting than the Brandenburg Gate?' Edith said.

'It's not about how interesting it is. The Holocaust Memorial is an important monument honouring a desperately tragic event in history.'

'Hang on a second,' Frank stood up and stretched his back. 'You said that Road School was all about following the kids' interests.'

'Oh do be quiet.' I zipped up the backpack and handed it to Frank.

We walked towards the Holocaust Memorial. I had no idea of what to expect, and when we got there it was nothing like I would have expected if I'd had an idea of what to expect. The monument filled a large square to one side of the Brandenburg Gate. It was made up of thousands of large grey concrete slabs of different sizes. There were spaces between the slabs. The whole area sloped down towards the centre of the square.

'This is more like it!' Edith ran off into the jumble of concrete blocks.

'Wait for me!' Alfie chased after her.

'Kids!' I shouted after my disappearing children. 'Don't run! It's not a play area, you know!' Within seconds I had lost sight of both of them. They had disappeared somewhere inside the huge forest of concrete. I looked at Frank. Frank looked at me.

'I'll go and see where they've gone and get them to behave a bit more appropriately,' I said.

'I'll stay here with the bags.' Frank slumped down on a bench and looked longingly across the road. The Beer Tour of Berlin was passing slowly by; German music was blaring from a giant loud-speaker perched on the roof of the rickshaw. The tourists were downing beers, singing rowdy songs and laughing loudly.

The architect Peter Eisenman and the engineer Buro Happold designed the Holocaust Memorial. It is made up of 2,711 concrete stelae which are arranged on a sloping site. As you enter the field of slabs, you go downhill – the idea was apparently to create a sense of being confused and off balance, to show how a supposedly ordered society can lose touch with human reason. I tottered off downhill into the centre of the memorial in search of the kids. The stelae are set in a grid pattern. Every so often I would see one of my children run past in one direction. Shortly afterwards I would see the other child run past in the opposite direction. It was like being trapped in a maze. Every time I got to the corner of one of the blocks I would look in one direction, then the other, but the children were nowhere to be seen. Then, just as I moved on to the edge of the next slab, I would see one of the kids whiz past out of the corner of my eye.

Eventually I gave up and made my way back uphill and out of the maze of blocks. Frank was still sitting on the bench. He was reading the European edition of the *Sunday Times*.

'No luck, then?' He looked up.

I slumped down beside him. 'No luck.'

'We could just leave them to it and take the beer tour?' There was a hint of longing in Frank's eyes and a distinct note of hope in his voice.

Just at that moment, Edith and Alfie came charging out of the labyrinth of grey slabs.

'We're hungry!' Edith said.

'And thirsty!' Alfie said.

'Can we have an ice cream?' Edith wanted to know. 'I'm planning to become a connoisseur of ice cream.'

'Okay,' I said. 'Then afterwards we can visit Checkpoint Charlie.'

'Maybe I could do the beer tour while you …' I stopped Frank mid-sentence with a swift elbow to the ribs.

Edith looked at her father and raised her eyebrows. 'Don't be such a philistine, daddy.'

Fame

The Museum für Naturkunde, Berlin's natural history museum, was a treasure trove of natural wonders. There were beautiful crystals and amazing creatures. There was a fantastic interactive solar system exhibit. And there was a very strange room full of dead things preserved in jars, like something out of a horror movie. But according to our dinosaur-obsessed son, the museum was amazing mainly because it was home to the 'most famous fossil in the world'. When I said that we were going to follow our children's interests during our Road School trip, what I probably should have mentioned was that one of Alfie's interests has always been dinosaurs. He falls in and out of love with them on a three year cycle. At that moment he was in an 'I love dinosaurs' period, with palaeontologist right at the top of his list of 'things I will do to earn money when I'm older'.

Alfie first got into dinosaurs when he was 3 years old. In those days it was mainly about stroking pictures of cartoon-like dinosaurs in the Usborne *That's Not My Dinosaur* book and reading every title in the 'Harry and His Bucketful of Dinosaurs' series. He fell out of love with dinosaurs for a while, but by the age of 6 he was back into them again, and this time round he was old enough to appreciate the fossils at the Natural History Museum in London. We spent countless hours trudging round and round the dinosaur exhibits while he soaked up all the knowledge that he could. We bought never-ending dinosaur related toys and books, and Alfie began his life's mission to memorise all their names. He then fell back out of love with them, only to fall back in love again at the age of 9. By this stage it was all about the names and the details and the facts. A set of Top Trumps cards helped, but it was a massive book called *Dinosaurs* by Michael Benton and Steve Brusatte that sealed the deal. When I ordered the book, I didn't quite realise the size of it. It wasn't actually delivered by crane, but it felt like it should have been.

Alfie stood in front of the *Archaeopteryx* exhibit and drooled. He touched his fingers to the glass and peered in wonder at the fossil trapped behind it.

'Are you okay, son?' Frank looked a bit worried. There was no reply from Alfie.

'Is he okay?' Frank turned to me with a puzzled look on his face.

'I think he's having a star-struck moment,' I said.

'Star-struck?' Frank raised his eyebrows.

'This is the most famous fossil in the world,' Alfie finally turned round and addressed his dad in an awestruck voice. 'It's the biggest celebrity of the fossil world. It's worth millions of pounds. And I'm in the same room as it. My life is complete.'

The 'Berlin specimen' of *Archaeopteryx* was discovered in the late nineteenth century, not long after Charles Darwin had written his famous book *On the Origin of Species*. It is the most complete specimen of *Archaeopteryx* ever found, although the guy who discovered it obviously didn't realise how important it was because in 1876 he sold it and bought a cow with the money instead. If he'd known the impact it would have on our son, almost 150 years later, he might have set a slightly higher price.

Way Down in the Hole

After Berlin, our next destination was Frankfurt. To get from Berlin to Frankfurt we had to go from the top right to the bottom left of Germany. And as we took our long diagonal route across the country, we were going to pass through a small region called the Harz. During my pre-trip research, I had discovered that the Harz has the tallest mountain range in northern Germany. The highest peak in the range is called the Brocken, and there are all kinds of stories about witches and other strange creatures associated with the mountain. There are also plenty of caves in this part of the country, and I had planned for us to visit the two most famous ones. We were going down in a hole to see the wonders that lurked beneath our feet.

There was drizzle in the air as we drove into the village of Rübeland, where the two caves known as Baumannshöhle and Hermannshöhle are located. *The Rough Guide to Germany* had recommended these caves for their 'stunning Devonian limestone formations'. The caves were only a few miles from the apartment where we were stopping over for the night, so it seemed like a great plan to drop in and see them on the way. We parked up and made our way along the road towards the entrance as light rain began to fall.

We booked our tickets for the tour. It was lunchtime, and the next tour wasn't until 2 p.m., so we had an hour to kill. However, as in tourist destinations around the world, there were plenty of things for the children to do while we waited for our visit to begin. Which roughly translates as 'there was plenty of tat on sale that would suck the money out of us because our children wouldn't stop whinging until we bought it for them'. There was, of course, a shop selling crystals, although most of the crystals on sale didn't seem to have come from anywhere near Germany. According to the kids, there was also a machine that made coins. They jumped up and down in excitement as they informed us of this fact.

'A machine that makes coins?' Frank sounded at once sceptical and intrigued.

'I need a euro and a five cent piece to make my coin,' Edith said.

'So do I,' Alfie said.

'Ah. A machine that makes coins by taking coins away from you.' Frank looked disappointed. He fished in his pocket and handed the kids a euro and a five cent piece each.

A few minutes later, Edith ran back over holding an oval shaped copper coin and looking thrilled. 'The machine stamped a bear on my coin!'

'And on mine!' Her brother held his coin out for inspection.

'They have bears in this part of Germany?' I gulped nervously.

'Can we buy some crystals now?' the kids chorused. Frank reached into his pocket again.

An hour later, a lot of souvenirs heavier and thirty euros lighter, it was time for our tour to begin. We crossed a long bridge and stopped at a heavy door. The guide opened the door and one by one we picked our way down some steep rocky steps. All around us there were stalactites and stalagmites, created over the millennia by the dripping water.

'Which ones are stalactites and which ones are stalagmites?' Edith wanted to know.

'Not a clue,' I said. 'Frank?' Frank shook his head.

Luckily Alfie came to our rescue. 'Stalactites hang on tight to the ceiling, while stalagmites might grow up to meet them some day,' he explained.

'Cool.' Edith started singing Alfie's saying to herself. Loudly.

'Shut up,' Alfie said.

'No.' His sister carried on singing. 'Stalactites hang on tight to the ceiling, while stalagmites might grow up to meet them some day.'

Among the many famous visitors to the show caves of Rübeland was the German writer and statesman Johann Wolfgang von Goethe. About halfway through our tour of the caves we reached the huge chamber known as the Goethesaal, which is named after Goethe, and in which theatre performances are now hosted. There was a large shallow lake on one side of the cave with stalagmites sticking up from under the water – strange alien shapes in the shadowy half-light. Water dripped down from the roof of the cave and made a plopping sound as it hit the still surface of the lake. On the far side of the pool was a raised platform that was used as the stage.

'In a moment I am going to turn off all the lights,' the tour guide told us. 'When this happens, it will be very dark.'

'Talk about stating the obvious,' I whispered to Edith.

'I'm not afraid of the dark, mummy.' She grabbed my hand and squeezed it.

The guide flicked off the lights, and suddenly we realised what he meant by 'very dark'. The darkness was so thick that it felt like you could reach out and touch it. Where we live, in the Somerset countryside, it can get pretty dark at night, but this was a totally different kind of darkness. The world had disappeared to be replaced by a thick, inky black that invaded the senses and seemed to press down on you from all sides. All around me, I heard intakes of breath from the rest of our group. Edith was crushing my hand so tightly that it had begun to lose all sensation.

A few minutes later the guide turned the lights back on, and we all blinked like moles coming up out of the darkness. Edith let go of my hand and I shook it to try to get some feeling back into it.

The final series of caves held a surprise: a bear-shaped skeleton surprise. According to the guide, the Baumannshöhle bear died when it was hibernating and some rocks fell on it. This was the reason why our kids now had coins in their pockets with a bear stamped on them.

'Woah,' Alfie said, 'that is amazing.' He leaned over the rail and peered at the bear skeleton. 'Imagine being trapped down here forever.' He turned to his sister and used his best spooky voice: 'Trapped in the darkness, crushed by rocks, unable to escape from the inky blackness.'

'Mum, he's scaring me. Make him stop.' Edith's voice wobbled.

About an hour after we had entered the caves, we stumbled out of the exit and into the fading afternoon light. All the time we were underground it felt like we had been going down, down, down into the depths of the earth. I had convinced myself that we were deep below the surface. In my mind, we had visited the bowels of the planet. But suddenly here we were – blinking in the daylight – and we were high up on a hillside. How on earth had that happened? We stood there for a moment, our eyes adjusting to the daylight. Far below us we could see the entrance to Baumannshöhle and the car park where we had left our car a few hours earlier. It felt like we had visited another world – a world full of nature's mysteries, hidden from view in the dark. A world that was under our feet all the time, even though we were unaware of it. It was fascinating and beautiful way down in the hole, but I was glad to be back in the light.

A Hazy Shade of Winter

As we arrived at the apartment in Braunlage where we were staying the night, it started to snow heavily. Edith and Alfie both squealed with delight.

'Daddy, daddy! It's snowing!' Edith said.

'Let's have a snowball fight,' Alfie grabbed a handful of snow and chucked it at his sister. She screamed and started crying.

'Great,' Frank said. We dragged our suitcases inside and went to check in.

'I hit the jackpot this time, Frank.' I smiled as we were shown around a large, spacious apartment. This was definitely the best accommodation of our trip so far.

'Shame we're only staying one night in it, then. Especially since we're in a separate bedroom to the children.' Frank winked at me. 'I think you should get an early night, kids.'

'I'm not tired yet, daddy,' Edith said.

'Me neither.' Alfie switched on the TV and starting flicking through the channels in search of an inappropriate programme to watch.

'Well, me and your mum are having an early night, isn't that right?' Frank did the wink thing again and smiled at me lecherously. He did a weird kind of waggling finger gesture in the direction of the bedroom.

'I'm not tired either yet, Frank.' I raised my eyebrows. It was, after all, only five o'clock in the afternoon.

We woke up the next morning to a blanket of white. Snow sat heavy on the wooden roofs. The car was covered in several inches of snow. Frank had a happy smile on his face, though, thanks to the separate bedrooms (although he looked slightly wistful that we weren't staying longer).

Before we set off for Frankfurt, we just had time to do a bit more local sightseeing in the Harz. The car park at the gondola lift on the other side of Braunlage was almost deserted. At this time of year the skiers were long gone. We climbed out of the car and hurried towards the building, a biting wind tearing at our clothes. There were only a handful of other tourists inside. We bought our tickets and waited for the next cable car to make its way down the mountain towards us. As it reached the bottom the doors swung open and we stepped inside.

'You sit there,' Edith said to Frank, pointing to the backward-facing seat. 'Mummy, you sit here between us.' We dropped into our seats, the door slammed shut and the car made its way up the steep incline. All around us, the slopes were covered in pine and fir trees. The snow was still falling. The higher we got up the mountain, the thicker it had settled on the ground. Fifteen minutes later we reached the top of the Wurmberg, the second highest mountain in the Harz. The door of the cable car slid open and we jumped out. Up here it was even colder and the snow was thick on the ground. We seemed to be the only people venturing outside that day. We zipped up our coats tightly and pulled on our hats and gloves. Then we headed out into the snowy wilderness.

'Have a look at this.' Frank called me over to where he was studying an information board about the Wurmberg. 'This mountain was on the border between West and East Germany during the Cold War. The US secret services built a listening tower here in 1972 to monitor signals from East Germany.'

'Oww!' A large snowball smacked Frank in the back of the head. We turned around to see Alfie and Edith standing behind us armed with snowballs. 'What do you think you're doing?'

'We're re-enacting the Cold War, daddy,' Edith said.

'What do you mean?' I said.

'We're at war with you!' Alfie lobbed another snowball at his dad.

'And you're going to get cold!' Edith's snowball slapped into the side of my face. I felt an icy, wet sensation as snow trickled down my cheek. The two kids ran off to a safe distance to make more snowballs. Frank and I bent down and fashioned some snowballs of our own. And then we celebrated our visit to the Harz, there on the border of a once divided nation, with a massive family snowball fight.

Don't Look Back in Anger

One of the things that Frank really wanted to do on our tour of Europe was go to Frankfurt. This was not because he is named after the city (he isn't) but because he lived there when he was a kid. Frank is far more widely travelled than me; as a child he had family in exotic places – Angola, India, Portugal, Jersey. (That's Jersey in the

Channel Islands, rather than Jersey in North America, so it's not exactly exotic, but you get the idea.) We had now reached the bit of our journey where Frank got to look back in time and reminisce about where he used to live when he was a child. It was Frank's very own midlife crisis moment. But before he could do that, we had to spend at least an hour driving around in circles trying to locate the house where he used to live when he was a child, in a small town on the outskirts of Frankfurt called Kronberg im Taunus.

'It's definitely around here somewhere.'

'Can you be a bit more specific than "around here somewhere"?' I sighed. 'I can't exactly plug "around here somewhere" into the satnav. Do you have an address?' Frank ignored me.

'Can we go to the hotel yet?' Edith said. We had been on the road all day, and the children were tired and hungry.

'Not yet.' I stifled a yawn. 'We just have to drive around for ages looking for your father's old house first.'

'Maybe it's down here,' Frank made a sudden left turn across the oncoming traffic. Car horns blared at us. 'It doesn't look anything like it used to when we were kids. There were orchards and trees and open farmland, not roads and buildings and concrete.'

'Why don't you phone your mother and ask her what the name of your road was? Then I can put the address into the satnav.'

'I'll find it in a minute. It's definitely around here somewhere.'

Frank does not like asking his mother for help. He likes his independence, even if it means tormenting me and the kids.

'Can I phone your mother and ask her?'

'No.' Frank's tone told me he wasn't going to change his mind.

'Hey, kids, look! That's the Montessori school where I used to go when I was 9! And look, that was our local swimming pool!' The kids lifted their heads momentarily from their electronic devices and made a vague attempt to look interested in their dad's trip down memory lane.

'Are we going to get to the hotel soon?' Alfie said. 'I'm hungry.'

'Mum says there's a swimming pool at the hotel,' Edith said. 'And a sauna. I can't wait to go in the sauna. I've never been in a sauna before.'

'This won't take long. Ah! Now this looks familiar! Maybe it's along here.' Frank cut down a small road on our right.

'There it is!' Frank had a broad grin on his face. He drove to the end of a narrow road and pointed at a nondescript looking house. 'This is where I used to live when I was a child, kids.'

'Great.' The kids didn't even look up from their consoles.

'And around the back here was an orchard.' Frank drove past the house and turned to the right where the road seemed to come to a dead end. 'If we go down here I'll be able to show you the balcony where me and my brother used to set off fireworks.'

'Oh,' I said as we rounded the corner. 'It's not an orchard any more then.'

A massive building site stretched away from us into the distance. Diggers crisscrossed the space, beeping as they reversed. They scraped up earth and moved it from one place to another. The fruit trees were gone. The orchard was no more. It only existed in Frank's memory now. I looked at Frank. He had a wistful, sad look in his eyes.

'It's all gone.' I might have been imagining it, but I think Frank's voice cracked slightly with emotion at that point.

I took his hand and gave it a squeeze. 'The past is a foreign country, Frank,' I said. 'They do things differently there.'

Hot In the City

When I was a kid, I didn't live in Germany, like Frank did. I didn't go on holiday to Portugal every year, like Frank did. And I didn't have relatives in exotic places such as India or Angola either, like Frank did. I did, however, have a mostly absent father who travelled the world for his job. I would regularly receive postcards from exciting sounding European cities and letters from exotic sounding places in Africa. When I got a guinea pig, I decided to name it after the place where my dad was staying at the time. And at the point when I got my guinea pig, he happened to be working in a place called Bad Homburg, on the outskirts of Frankfurt. And so it was that I called my guinea pig 'Humbug' (he was the colour of a humbug sweet as well.) It was this childhood memory which meant that, when I was looking for accommodation in Frankfurt, I decided that we should stay in Bad Homburg. If Frank was going to revisit his childhood memories of Frankfurt, then I was damn well going to revisit my second-hand memories as well.

After our scenic tour of the outskirts of Frankfurt, we made our way to our hotel and checked in. I had picked this particular hotel because it had a pool and a sauna. The kids were excited – although they had been swimming a lot in their lives, they had never been to a sauna before.

'We're going to suss out the pool and the sauna,' I said. 'Do you want to come?' Frank shook his head and carried on tapping numbers into his spreadsheet. I think he was still a bit traumatised by his trip down memory lane. I went with the kids in the lift, down to the pool. After a quick swim we were ready to go into the sauna. The kids hurried ahead while I gathered our belongings together.

'Mum!' Alfie was peeking through the window into the steamy room.

'What?'

Edith went up on tiptoes and peeked through the window too. 'OMG. There are naked men in there.' Her eyes went wide and her mouth dropped open.

'They've got all their bits hanging out,' Alfie said.

'It's disgusting,' Edith said.

'I'm not going in *there*,' Alfie said.

'Stop being such prudes. I'm sure it's fine. People always take their clothes off in a sauna. Shift over and let me have a look.' I was quite keen on the idea of seeing some gorgeous German men sweating naked in a sauna. I peered in through the window and wrinkled my nose.

'Urggh. That guy is 80 years old if he's a day. Let's get out of here and go tell your father.'

'Did you have a good time in the pool?' Frank looked up from his laptop as we came back into the room.

'The pool was great,' Alfie said.

'But the sauna was *disgusting*,' Edith said.

'What do you mean, it was disgusting? Was it dirty or something?

That's not very Germanic. They're normally obsessive about cleanliness in Germany.'

'No. It wasn't dirty,' Alfie said. 'There were *naked men* in there.'

'They had *no clothes on at all*, daddy.' Edith still hadn't erased the look of horror from her face.

Frank looked at me and raised an eyebrow. 'Naked men, eh?' he said. 'I bet your mother wasn't too upset about that.'

'Frank,' I said, 'they were not only naked. They were ancient.'

'Yeah. Their skin was all wrinkly and gross,' Edith said.

'Welcome to Germany. Nudity is part of the culture here. Just wait until we visit a spa with your German cousins. We'll all have to get naked then.' Frank turned to me. He had a broad smile on his face.

'*Yuk!*' the kids said, wrinkling their noses.

'Don't get your hopes up,' I said.

'A man can dream, can't he?' Frank said.

Once In a Lifetime

One of the most vivid memories I had of my childhood tour of Europe was the castle at Neuschwanstein, in the south-west corner of the state of Bavaria, not far from Munich. The castle lived on in my mind as a kind of Disneyland-style extravaganza. The blues of the turrets were amazing. The steep walk up to the castle was long and winding and mysterious. Inside the castle there was gold, jewels and extravagantly decorated rooms. I remembered the story of mad King Ludwig II who had commissioned the castle, higher up the mountain than the one that his father had built before him. The entire experience had burned itself into my memory in a series of never-to-be-forgotten images that captured the place perfectly. Or so I thought.

After touring the sights of Frankfurt, we were spending the last part of our visit to Germany with Frank's German cousin, Helmut, his wife Monika and their three kids in their home in the town of Tutzing, near Munich. When we arrived at their house, we were surprised to discover that Frank's cousin had never visited Neuschwanstein Castle, despite living only a few miles away from it. We were also surprised to find out that they didn't have Wi-Fi.

'But you only live twenty minutes away from the castle,' I pointed out.

'And everyone needs access to the Internet,' Frank muttered under his breath.

'I suppose it is like anyone living near a famous tourist attraction,' Helmut said. 'You know it is there. But it is for the tourists. It is not for the normal people. But now we have an excuse to go. The children are very excited.'

The sky was grey and glowering as we wound our way along the roads between Tutzing and Neuschwanstein. There was a knot of excitement in my stomach. Would the castle look the same as it did in my memory? Could it possibly live up to the image that I had in my head from my childhood? Suddenly I spotted something off in the distance that looked a bit like a castle, although a rather dull and uninspiring one if I was being honest about it. The castle was perched on the side of a low hill.

'I think that might be it,' I said.

'I thought you said you'd been here before?' Frank said. 'Don't you remember what it looks like?'

'Let's wait until we get a bit closer.' I tried to hide my disappointment. Where were the blue turrets? Where was the snow-capped mountain? Where was the winding pathway to the top? Had my memory deceived me, or did things really look so very different when you were a child? Maybe the inside of the castle would chime with my childhood vision of gold, jewelled perfection. At least there was that.

Even though it was only mid-morning, the car park was already rammed with cars. We squeezed into parking spaces and convened to make a plan. There was a long queue to book tickets to see the inside of the castles – the line already stretched back from the ticket office to the car park.

'I bet we could have booked tickets online,' I whispered to Frank.

'Yeah, but that would involve actually having Wi-Fi,' Frank winked at me.

The adults assembled to discuss the problem and made an executive decision not to bother queuing for tickets to see the castle interiors. We had more important things to do that afternoon. Helmut had suggested that, after our visit to the castle, we should all go for a swim in a nearby spa. We were looking forward to it, although the kids were nervous about the whole nudity thing. Luckily for them I had packed our swimming costumes. I just hoped Helmut had packed some for him and his three kids as well.

We walked past the father's castle at the bottom of the hill and began to make our way up to the top to see the son's one. A horse and cart clip clopped its way past us. It was full of tourists. They looked very happy to be ascending the hill in comfort rather than trailing up the steep slope with the rest of us.

'Look, it's a horse and cart! Can we go up in the horse and cart?' the five kids shouted simultaneously.

'No,' said Frank.

'Nein,' said Helmut.

'Meanies,' Alfie said.

'Aww … why not?' Edith said.

'Because euros,' Frank said.

'And PE,' I added.

The road up to the castle was long, steep and winding, and covered in steaming piles of horseshit. As we climbed, picking our way around the horse poo, we were overtaken by a series of slow moving horses and carts. Each time one passed us, the cry went up again from the children. 'Can we go up in the horse and cart?' but the adults remained resolute. We caught glimpses of the castle as we ascended the hill. The dull grey turrets peeked out from above the trees. Eventually we came to a viewpoint where we stopped to catch our breath.

'Wow,' Edith gazed up at the castle with a dreamy look in her eyes. 'It looks like something out of a Disney fairy tale.' Perhaps, I thought, everything just looks better when you're 8 years old.

'Actually, it is like something out of a Disney fairy tale,' Frank said.

'Yeah, right.' I was deeply sceptical about my dreams of Disney by this point.

'No, seriously. Neuschwanstein Castle was the inspiration for the Sleeping Beauty Castle at the Disneyland Theme Park. It was also used in the movies *Chitty Chitty Bang Bang* and *The Great Escape.*' Frank was proving to be a repository of fascinating but irrelevant facts.

'I can see why. It's beautiful.' Edith gave a blissful sigh. We carried on up the hill until we reached the top, then we made our way in through the impressive entrance gates. There was another long queue of tourists lining up to go inside the castle. I looked wistfully at the queue, but reminded myself that the inside of the castle would probably have been a disappointment as well.

The kids were busy anticipating the spa with a mixture of nervousness and excitement. 'Will the people in there be naked?' Alfie wanted to know.

'This is very likely,' Helmut said. 'German people like to get naked when they go to a spa.'

'Will *we* have to get naked too?' Alfie said.

'Well, that is up to you. But it is lovely to feel the hot water on your naked body.' Helmut smiled at the thought.

'That's disgusting!' Edith said.

'Oh, it is quite normal here in Germany,' he said. 'Is this not the same in your country?'

'Definitely not,' Alfie said.

'Germans are weird,' Edith hissed under her breath.

'Sssh,' I hissed back at her.

We headed back downhill, got in our cars and left the castle behind. As we drove across town to the thermal pool, it began to snow. Instantly, the dull grey German landscape was transformed into something beautiful. It's amazing how snow does that. As we parked up at the spa, fat snowflakes dropped heavily onto our cars and immediately began to settle. We paid our entrance fee, got changed into our swimsuits and made our way into the spa. Thankfully Helmut and his children had decided to wear swimming costumes too. Pretty much everyone else in the spa had not.

'The people in here are all naked,' Edith muttered. 'Again.'

'Look at the size of that guy's willy.' Alfie pointed at a man who was walking down the steps into the hot pool.

'Woah,' Frank said. 'I hope your mum doesn't see that and get any ideas.'

'Frank!' I slapped him on the arm.

The spa had a variety of hot pools – some indoors and some outdoors. The warm water was wonderfully relaxing. We swam from the first indoor pool through to the second one, and our jaws dropped open in surprise. There were bar stools *in* the pool, and there were people sitting on them. Naked. They were drinking beer, cocktails and champagne in a hot swimming pool.

'This is weird,' I said to Frank. 'There are naked German people sitting on bar stools in hot water drinking beer.'

'Oh I don't know. I quite fancy a beer, and I'll happily get naked to drink it if you do,' Frank said.

'Daddy!' Edith sounded horrified.

'Don't even *think* about it!' Alfie said.

From the indoor pool, we swam through a plastic curtain into the hot pool outside. This pool was great fun because it had a swirling current that carried you rapidly round and round a central island. The children whooped with delight, and chased each other around the island. I found a quiet spot at the edge and pulled Frank towards me for a kiss, savouring the moment.

We looked across the valley floor towards the mountain, where mad King Ludwig's castle perched on the rocky heights. It looked a hell of a lot better from this angle, in the hot water, with the snow starting to settle on it. The snow began to fall faster and faster until it began to obscure the castle from view. Huge fat flakes drifted down and landed on our eyelashes. It was the strangest sensation – the contrast between the heat of the water and the freezing cold snow. We kept blinking to try to clear the snowflakes from our eyelashes, but as fast as we cleared them off, more replaced them. I thought back over the day, and how my childhood memories had deceived me.

I turned to Frank. 'I've decided something.'

'What's that?' he said, wiping a particularly large snowflake off my nose.

'Even though I didn't find the castle in the air with blue turrets from my childhood, I discovered something even better.'

'And that is?'

'Snowflakes that stay on my nose and eyelashes. It's like being in a version of *The Sound of Music*.' I gave him another kiss, longer this time.

'Will you two stop being so soppy and come and swim with us!' Edith said, as the current dragged her past the spot where we were sitting. I gave Frank one more kiss and then I followed her, diving under the water and letting the heat of the pool melt the snow that had settled in my hair.

'This is amazing, mummy!' Edith said, as I resurfaced.

'Isn't it just?' I smiled. 'Isn't it just?'

'I'm going to bring my children here when I'm grown up,' she said. 'So that they can see how magical it is too.'

Bring On the Dancing Horses

'Tomorrow we're going to the circus!' Helmut announced.

'Cool,' Edith said.

'Excellent,' Alfie said.

'Is it in Munich?' I said.

'Oh no,' Helmut told us. 'It is here in Tutzing. The circus visits Tutzing every year.'

'Is it any good?' Frank said.

'Oh yes. Everyone loves it when the circus comes to Tutzing. It is one of the highlights of the year.' Frank looked at me sceptically.

I've always loved the idea of running away to join the circus, of travelling from place to place, of a life on the road. But while I've always loved the idea of it, the long term reality is probably not something I could handle. After a few weeks of Road School, I was starting to understand my limitations on the travel front.

'What do you reckon?' I asked Frank, as we climbed into bed that night. 'Do you think this circus will be any good?'

'I wouldn't get your hopes up.'

The next day we walked through Tutzing to the small park where the circus was being held, and queued up at a booth to buy our tickets. The park bordered a lake where Frank's cousin and his family swam each summer.

'This had better be good,' Frank whispered to me as we approached the circus tent. 'It certainly cost enough.'

The scruffy red and yellow tent had been erected on some scrubby parkland. It didn't exactly fill me with optimism. We pushed aside the tent flaps and made our way inside. There were three rows of uncomfortable looking metal seats arranged in a semi-circle with a wooden barrier in front of them. Beyond that was a small circus ring area. A single limp looking trapeze hung from the roof, swaying backwards and forwards in the draught.

'Urrggh! This tent smells of horse poo.' Edith made the announcement a bit too loudly for comfort.

'It's not exactly Cirque du Soleil, is it?' I said to Frank. I was rapidly readjusting my expectations downwards.

The show began. Two circus performers entered the ring. One of them was leading a small horse; the other one was carrying a stool. The horse had brown and white patches on it and a dog-eared red blanket over its back. It looked distinctly unimpressed and unimpressive. For the first part of the show, we were treated to the sight of the small brown and white horse dancing around in circles in the ring. Occasionally it would stop, put its front feet up onto the stool and pause. The German audience clapped loudly in apparent delight. Then off the little horse would go again. After about ten minutes of this the kids were starting to get restless. The metal seat was digging into my bum.

'Is it going to get more exciting soon?' Edith yawned.

'Yes,' I said. 'And ssshh.' I put a hand over her mouth to stop her protesting. 'You mustn't be rude. Your cousins are enjoying it.'

'It is a bit crap, mum,' Alfie pointed out.

'Ssshh,' I said. Helmut turned around. I smiled at him and put my other hand over Alfie's mouth.

'It is okay?' he said. 'You are enjoying our circus here in Tutzing?'

'Oh yes, it's great. The kids were just saying how much they were enjoying it.' I grinned at Frank's cousin. 'Weren't you, kids?' The kids nodded. I removed my hands from their mouths. It wouldn't do to suffocate them.

After a few more circuits the white and brown horse limped out of the ring, looking worn out. Next it was the turn of a larger brown horse with a feathered red headdress. The brown horse did a few circuits of the ring. Then one of the circus performers hopped up onto its back and began to juggle.

'See, I told you it would get better in a bit,' I smiled at the kids.

'This is better?' Alfie had a disbelieving look on his face.

Next a man entered with a stack of four white wooden stools.

'What's he going to do with those?' Edith wanted to know.

'Balance them on his chin by the look of it,' I said, as the man balanced the first stool on his chin.

'This is even more boring than the horses running round in rings,' Alfie said. Moments later the chin-stool-balancer had reached the lofty heights of a whole four stools balanced on his chin. He exited, and everyone in the audience stood up and applauded.

'Is that it?' Edith was incredulous.

'Do not worry, Edith,' Helmut said. 'This is just the half-time break. There will be more amazing excitement after. We will go and get some delicious refreshments.'

We wandered out of the tatty tent to stretch our legs.

'Daddy, daddy,' Edith tugged at Frank's sleeve.

'What?' Frank said.

'Candyfloss.' The drool ran down Edith's chin as she pointed towards a wizened old lady selling blue candyfloss.

'Not a chance,' Frank said. 'That stuff rots your teeth. And I spent all my cash on the tickets for this circus.'

'This is okay,' Helmut's wife Monika said. 'I will buy the children a candyfloss.'

Frank's mouth dropped open. His cousin's family were the organic, free range, eco-friendly, no food colourings, water-drinking kind of people. The candyfloss was the most lurid colour you could imagine. Five minutes later Edith poked out her tongue at Frank. It was bright blue.

'Come on children, the second half is about to start,' Helmut waved to us from over by the tent. The children trudged unwillingly back towards the marquee.

The circus had clearly saved all the good stuff for the second half. Well, perhaps 'good' was a bit of an exaggeration, but the second half was at least a bit more attention-grabbing than the first half had been. First up was a female trapeze artist wearing an outfit that consisted of three small scraps of leather stitched together. It barely covered her modesty, let alone anything else.

Frank smiled. 'This is more like it.' He leaned forwards to get a closer look.

The woman weaved and swung and twisted and twirled on the trapeze for five minutes, while all the men in the audience stared wide-eyed at her costume.

'I could get you one of those outfits if you like,' Frank said.

'Not a chance.'

Next up was the fire-eater. 'Ah, now this is better,' Alfie said.

'This is cool,' Edith said.

'Technically speaking it's not cool,' Frank pointed out. 'It's very hot.' Edith gave him a look.

'If there's petrol in his mouth,' Alfie said, 'why doesn't it explode?' There was a loud bang and the fire-eater's mouth appeared to explode. 'Oh, it does explode,' he said.

'I like this circus,' Edith smiled widely.

'So do I,' Alfie grinned.

'And me,' Frank joined in. 'The trapeze artist was the best bit. Her costume was superb.'

I was definitely going to have to wipe the grin off Frank's face later.

Karma Police

The next bit of our Road School adventure was going to take place in Italy, but in order to get to Italy from Munich we had to drive through Austria. To drive through Austria we had to buy a special sticker called a vignette. And even though we would only be in Austria for sixty miles, we still had to buy the sticker.

'I am not paying eight euros for ten days' travel on Austrian motorways just to cut through Austria on my way to Italy,' Frank announced.

'Oh, but you must pay,' Helmut said. 'I did not pay once and I got a big fine.'

'They can't fine us if they can't find us,' Frank said.

'Oh, but they will find you,' Frank's cousin insisted. 'You must be sure of this. And then they will make you pay the fine in cash.'

'They can't make me pay in cash if I don't have any.'

'Frank. If you do not have any cash, they will accompany you to a bank so you can get some,' Helmut said. 'And they will fine you even more because they had to spend their time taking you to the bank machine.'

Frank was keen to take a punt and not buy the vignette. We spent the rest of the evening having a blazing row about it as I shoved clothes angrily into suitcases and began to load the car, ready for the next part of our journey.

'It's Easter Sunday tomorrow. There is no way that there are going to be any traffic police around checking whether or not foreign drivers have got a vignette.'

'Frank. Just buy the bloody thing.'

'Mummy!' Edith said. 'Will you please stop swearing.'

'I don't even know where we can buy it,' Frank said. 'And it's not like I can check where to get one on the Internet.' He was still annoyed about the lack of Wi-Fi at his cousin's house.

The next morning we set off early from Tutzing. I chewed at a nail nervously as we drew closer and closer to the Austrian border.

'What if we don't find anywhere to buy the vignette?' I said to Frank.

'Then we won't buy the damn thing.'

'Will you *please* stop swearing, daddy?' Alfie piped up from the back seat.

'What's a vignette?' Edith wanted to know.

Half a mile from the Austrian border I spotted a sign. 'Look! You can buy one here.' I pointed to a garage on the side of the road with a big sign outside. Frank pulled into the garage forecourt and parked up. Then he disappeared, huffing and puffing, into the shop.

'Why is daddy taking so long?' Edith asked me, ten minutes later.

'I'm hungry,' Alfie said. The back floor of the car was littered with empty biscuit packets. The kids had already powered through all the snacks that I had packed for them.

'You'll just have to wait,' I checked my watch. 'It's only 12.30. We should be through Austria and into Italy in plenty of time for lunch.'

Twenty minutes later, Frank returned from the garage shop, swearing under his breath about 'sodding queues'. He handed me a red sticker, started up the engine and did a wheel spin in his haste to get back on the road. I peeled the backing off the sticker and attached it to the centre of the windscreen, seconds before we crossed into Austria.

'What a waste of money that was,' Frank was still huffing and puffing.

'Err, Frank,' I pointed to the side of the road. A policeman was standing there, peering closely at the windscreen of each of the cars that had just driven through the border into Austria. A little way further up the road, a policewoman had stopped a car with a French number plate and was having an intense conversation with the driver.

'I told you so!' I felt triumphant. I had just saved Frank from being fined 250 euros.

By the time we reached Italy, it was two minutes before 2 p.m. The kids were whining non-stop about being starving hungry and asking when lunch was, over and over again. Frank was equally stressed about his empty stomach.

'Right. Lunch. This'll do.' Frank swerved into the car park of the first restaurant that we came to. The restaurant served pizza. Alfie jiggled up and down in excitement. He loves pizza.

We all piled out of the car and pushed through the front door into the restaurant. The restaurant was packed. A sour looking waiter came over to us.

'Chiuso,' he grunted at us. 'Le due,' he tapped his watch.

I turned to Frank with a question in my eyes.

'Closed,' Frank translated.

'It doesn't look closed to me. It looks rammed.'

'It closes at 2 p.m. If you hadn't made me queue for half an hour for the vignette, we'd have got here in plenty of time.'

I didn't like to point out that if I hadn't made Frank queue for the vignette, we would currently be driving to a cashpoint in Austria to have 250 euros extracted from us by the Austrian traffic police. Frank doesn't take being confronted with the truth well, especially on an empty stomach.

It was the same story at the next three restaurants that we tried.

'Oh well, at least we brought plenty of snacks,' I told my family, as we all trailed dejectedly back towards the car. I climbed in and tossed a carrier bag full of cookies and crisps into the back seat. 'Venice, here we come.'

As we drove through the Dolomites, with the scent of cheese and onion crisps and chocolate chip cookies stinking out the car, Frank kept muttering about 'bad karma' under his breath. 'I hope the campsite in Venice is going to be better than the one in Amsterdam,' he said.

I bit my tongue. To be honest, the way things were going that day, I wasn't holding out much hope.

German Lessons

1   If you're spending any length of time in Germany, be prepared to get naked.

2   While you don't need to mention the war on a visit to Germany, you would be hard pushed to forget the history of the twentieth century while you are there.

3   Children see the world through different eyes. The things that feel special and important to us when we are small may seem ordinary to us when we grow up, so it's best to see as many things as you possibly can when you are young.

4   You can't stop time and preserve the past in aspic. Whether you like it or not, the world moves on despite, not because of, you.

5   Snow is wonderful. When it snows, what looked ordinary before suddenly looks amazing. The combination of cold snow and hot water is an experience not to be missed, although (unless you are German) you don't have to get naked to do it.

6   It's magical going underground into the world that exists beneath our feet. It's a world that it is very easy to forget about until you go to see it.

7   If you want to remember something long term, you need to create hooks for yourself to hang it on to. Thanks to Alfie, I will never forget that stalactites hang on tight to the ceiling, while stalagmites might grow up one day to meet them.

8   When children are tiny, they have a wide-eyed curiosity about the world around them. As they get older, this has a habit of disappearing. Road School was about trying to recapture that childlike curiosity we have about the world when we are small. It was a playful adventure, which would take twists and turns, according to what interested us.

9   It's amazing how much you come to rely on having access to the Internet, and how much you miss it when you don't.

10 If you ever drive through Austria to Italy, buy a vignette. And remember that restaurants in the Dolomites close promptly at 2 p.m.

Cultural Literacy

According to some educationalists, what children really need is more knowledge, and more knowledge of a specific kind. This argument was first put forward by an American professor called E. D. Hirsch, who wrote a book called *Cultural Literacy: What Every American Needs to Know*. Hirsch had a theory that children need to learn the kind of knowledge that will help them read and understand the *New York Times*. He called this knowledge 'cultural literacy' and he included a long list of it in his book (a list that was out of date the moment he finished writing it because culture has a habit of never standing still). If you're a teacher you may have heard of E. D. Hirsch, because when Michael Gove was education secretary he mentioned him frequently in his speeches. The current schools minister in England, Nick Gibb, is also a fan of Hirsch. If you're a parent, the debate about cultural literacy may have passed you by. However, if your children are at a state school, their curriculum is being affected by Hirsch's ideas, even if you are not aware of them. The curriculum reforms that took place when Michael Gove was secretary of state for education were influenced by Hirsch's theory of cultural literacy, and particularly the idea that children should study 'the best that has been thought and said'.

To an extent Hirsch was right. Knowledge is exactly what children need because it helps them to make sense of their world. But the debate is not really about whether children need knowledge, it's about what kind of knowledge they need, how they should get access to it and what they should do with that knowledge once they have it. Who gets to say what 'the best knowledge' actually is? Is it more important for 10-year-olds to be able to identify a fronted adverbial, or to write an imaginative story? Do we want our teenagers to study novels by dead white men, or are modern, ethnically diverse stories an important part of their cultural heritage? Should the history curriculum focus on the story of Britain, or is it better for us to take a global view? Do we want to incorporate up-to-date references into our children's education, or are the only things worth learning from the past?

In the twenty-first century, we can get hold of knowledge in all sorts of places. We can find it in books, on television and via the Internet. Knowledge has been democratised, and we don't necessarily have to go to school to get access to it. Suddenly our traditional views about what 'an education' is have been challenged. Is education about memorising facts, reciting poetry and knowing your times tables, or is it also about the ability to evaluate and work with what you know and come up with new ideas? Should we accept the status quo, or will we try something new?

During Road School, cultural literacy was about:

- Finding knowledge through exploring and doing, rather than through being taught facts.
- Learning about the world first hand, with our emotions and our senses, as well as our intellects.
- Discovering how different places in the world feel to us – what their atmosphere is like, in addition to pieces of factual information about them.
- Looking for historical knowledge by visiting the places where history happened, and thinking about how it would have felt to the people who experienced it.
- Seeing that people do things differently in different countries, and understanding that opinions about what is appropriate may be specific to a culture.
- Spending time with people from other cultures, and getting an insight into what their lives are like.
- Understanding that we live in a global world, and that travel allows us to widen our perspective and see other viewpoints.
- Sharing some bits of our family's personal history – the places we have lived and the music we have enjoyed.
- Exploring the culture of today, as well as the culture of the past, and seeing what links there are between the two.
- Showing our children that what we might consider 'the best' is an opinion, rather than a fact, and that their opinions matter too.
- Celebrating our children's cultural heritage and family background by spending time with family in other countries.

Personal knowledge of a place or an experience is a very special thing. It is the difference between someone telling you what flying in a plane is like and actually flying in one. Although you can know everything there is to know about what the experience of flying would be like, until you have experienced that moment of take-off you don't really understand it. The same goes for travelling to other countries. By experiencing different cultures at first hand, our hope was that our children would become more culturally literate in the widest possible sense of the word. When you educate your children yourself, you have the power to decide which bits of culture are important and which cultural experiences make a life worth living.

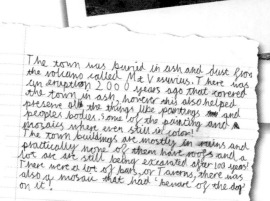

The town was buried in ash and dust from the volcano called Mt Vesuvius. There was an eruption 2000 years ago that covered the town in ash, however this also helped preserve all the things like paintings and peoples bodies. Some of the painting and mosaics where even still in color!
The town buildings are mostly in ruins and practically none of them have roofs and a lot are are still being excavated after 100 years! There were a lot of bars, or Taverns, there was also a mosaic that had 'beware of the dog' on it.

Next we went and got an ice-cream and went to an amazing fountain called Trevi. It is said that if you throw a coin in it you will come back to Rome. Around 3000 euro worth of coins is thrown in there everyday. many people have tried to steal from it. Then we walked down to the Spanish steps which for some reason are very popular even though I don't see anything special about it.

Next we went to the Colosseum. The Colosseum
was quite warn down but then it is 2000 years
old. The Colosseum is very big. It could have
50,000 people inside it. The gladiators fought wild
animals like lions, rhinos, elephants and hippos
They kept the animals underground until the
gladiators were ready to fight them. I bought a
snow globe of ~~Rome~~ Rome with my own money
it cost ~~euros~~.

Italy

Tower of Pisa

Today we went to Pisa to visit the leaning
tower of Pisa. In Italian it is called Torre
pendente. It was built in 1172. Did you know
that the leaning tower of Pisa was not built to
lean. It was built on marshland so it
sunk, and as it sunk it started ~~~~ leaning.
Now you can go up it but they only allow 40
people up at a time. To get up yere need to go
up 294 stairs.

Don't Fear the Reaper

As I had told Frank repeatedly before we set off on our Road School trip, we couldn't really go to Italy without visiting Venice. Frank had been decidedly lukewarm about the idea. It was the same story as with Paris: he had been to Venice when he was young; it was smelly and full of tourists; he didn't want to go there again. But, for me, Venice was part of my mission to revisit my childhood memories. And I wasn't about to revisit Italy without making a stopover in Venice. My Internet research had told me that hotels in Venice were hard to come by and expensive to stay in, and that parking close to a hotel was basically impossible. Happily, a quick chat with my mum before we set off revealed that there was another option. We could do what our family had done all those years before. It was possible to stay close to Venice on the Litorale del Cavallino, a peninsula that juts out from the mainland, enclosing the lagoon. Then we could take a boat across to Venice for the day.

Forty years earlier, my family had arrived at the Venetian campsite in our camper van. It was late at night when we got there, so we parked up quickly and settled straight down to sleep. But what we didn't realise was that there was a mosquito inside the camper van: a very hungry mosquito. In the morning I awoke to find that the mosquito had taken a liking to my face. One of my eyes was swollen shut, and would remain so for the rest of our time in Italy. To this day, I can remember exactly how it felt only being able to see Venice out of one eye. At least this time round I would get to see it with both eyes.

As we arrived at the campsite where we would be staying, Frank groaned. 'Not another shitty mobile home.'

'Language, daddy!' Edith frowned at him.

'Give it a chance,' I said. 'It might be better than the one in Amsterdam.'

We checked in and got our key, then we wove our way through the campsite towards our accommodation.

I jumped out of the car, determined to stall any complaints before they could even be voiced. I poked my head inside the mobile home and my heart sunk. If the mobile home in Amsterdam had been a bit of a problem, this one was a complete disaster. The seating area and the kitchen were tiny. Off to one side there was a tiny bedroom, with a bed that was just big enough for Frank, but only if he slept on it diagonally, and I slept on the floor. On the other side there were two miniscule bedrooms for the children in which the small single beds took up the entire space. There was a musty damp smell hanging in the air.

'How does it look?' Frank and the children wanted to know.

'Umm.' I paused and tried to conjure up some plus points. 'I don't think there are any mosquitoes. And it doesn't smell of poo. Oh and look, we have a lovely seating area outside,' I gestured hopefully at the scrubby area in front of the mobile home.

'Now I remember why I hate this place,' Frank told me, as we arrived by boat in Venice. There were hordes of tourists trudging slowly along the quay; people of all different nationalities, crushed together on the waterfront. We hopped off the boat and threaded ourselves into the mass of tourists walking towards Piazza San Marco. First up on our list of tourist destinations was St Mark's Basilica. It was free to go in, so Frank had happily agreed to a visit. We joined the queue of people waiting to go inside.

'Look, mummy,' Edith said a few minutes later, pointing behind me. A look of incomprehension was creeping across her face.

'Cool!' Alfie was looking over to where his sister had pointed. His eyes had opened wide.

I spun around to see what was going on. A scene from a horror movie was unfolding before me. A seagull had landed and it had a pigeon in its beak. As we watched, spellbound, the seagull dropped the injured pigeon to the ground.

'Oh that's okay then. The seagull has let the pigeon go.' I was relieved. I didn't want the children to witness a death in Venice, even if it only featured birds.

Just at that moment, the seagull reared backwards, wielding its beak like a weapon, and stabbed the pigeon three times. The pigeon shook; its body convulsed. Then it shuddered once and died. The seagull looked up. I could have sworn that it winked at me, although perhaps it was just a trick of the light. Then the seagull returned its attention to its prey. It began to devour the pigeon.

'Don't watch,' I stepped in front of the kids to try to block their view. I was unable to take my eyes off the scene. Alfie and Edith leaned around me so they could see. Their mouths had dropped open. They were riveted.

'This place is brilliant,' Alfie said.

'Amazing,' his sister agreed.

A mass of tourists heaved all around us, pushing and shoving as they made their way towards the Rialto Bridge.

'The Ponte di Rialto cost 19 million euros to build,' I read to the children from the guidebook as we trundled along with the rest of the crowd. 'It was designed by Antonio da Ponte and was completed in 1591.'

'I'm starving,' Edith moaned. 'Is it time for lunch yet?'

We had brought food with us in an attempt to avoid being ripped off by Venetian tourist prices, but there was literally nowhere to sit down, apart from outside an expensive cafe or restaurant. In a clever touch of fleece-the-tourists planning, the Venetians had made sure that, if you brought your own food, you were going to have to stand up to eat it.

'Let's eat our picnic here,' I shuffled sideways out of the heaving crush of tourists and headed closer to the canal. I fished into the backpack and pulled out some squashed sandwiches.

I'll admit that it wasn't the most salubrious place to eat. We were stuck between a giant green wheelie bin overflowing with rubbish, and the filthy, smelly Grand Canal. Just as I handed over the sarnies to my family, and we all took a hungry bite, a boat started up its engine beside us. A cloud of black exhaust fumes spewed into our faces.

Edith coughed loudly and waved both hands in front of her face, dropping her sandwich to the ground. A seagull swooped down and flew off with it.

'I told you that we shouldn't have bothered coming to Venice,' Frank said.

'The kids are enjoying it,' I said brightly. 'Aren't you kids?'

'Yeah,' Alfie smiled broadly. 'We saw a seagull murder a pigeon. Venice is great.'

Lean On Me

The next stop after Venice was Tuscany. And, clearly, since we were going to be spending some time in Tuscany, we had to visit the Leaning Tower of Pisa. To be honest, I was dreading it. What else could it possibly be but a disappointment, and a tourist rip-off to boot? The road up towards the Torre Pendente di Pisa was lined with stalls selling every kind of tourist tat you could imagine. There were small plastic Leaning Towers of Pisa, large pottery Leaning Towers of Pisa, medium sized neon Leaning Towers of Pisa. And, just in case you'd had your fill of Leaning Towers of Pisa, there were ridiculous sunglasses available for purchase as well.

Thankfully, as soon as we made it through the entrance into the Piazza dei Miracoli where the Leaning Tower was located, we left the tourist trappings far behind us. The cathedral complex was set inside the green space of a beautiful square. There was a large cathedral, its stone glowing white in the midday sun. Next to it was a large round baptistery, divided into tiers and looking distinctly like a giant white wedding cake, plonked there on the grass. And then there was the world famous bell tower with its distinctive lean. I was surprised at how pronounced the tilt was.

'It looks like it's going to fall over,' Alfie said.

'It does, doesn't it?' Frank agreed.

'I definitely wouldn't want to go up the top of that tower,' Edith said.

'That's a good thing,' I said, 'because I forgot to book tickets.'

We went to look more closely at the world famous Leaning Tower, and the kids studied the information boards set out in front of it. I looked around the green open space, and noticed that there was a spot on the immaculate lawns where all the tourists seemed to be gathering. I made my way over to see what they were doing, Edith dawdling along behind me. Lots of people were pointing cameras and taking snapshots of their companions with the Leaning Tower in the background.

'What are they doing?' Edith wanted to know.

'I'm not sure,' I peeked from behind one of the tourists to try to figure it out.

'Ah, I see.'

'What is it, mummy?'

'I'll tell you in a minute. Just go and stand over there for a sec.' I pointed to a spot on the grass in front of me. Edith headed over to where I was pointing. I checked through the viewfinder of the camera. 'Go right a tiny bit.' She shifted across a little bit more. 'That's perfect. Now stick your right arm out and put your hand straight up like this.' I demonstrated the perfect position.

'Why?' Edith wanted to know.

'Just do it and I'll show you afterwards. It's really funny, I promise you.' I snapped a few shots. 'Done,' I said. Edith hurried over to see what I had been doing.

'We're proper tourists today,' I told her, showing her the pictures I had just taken.

Edith giggled. 'It looks like I'm holding up the tower with my hand!' she was delighted. 'Daddy! Alfie! Come and have a look!' she shouted over to them. 'It looks like the Leaning Tower of Pisa is leaning on me!'

A Design for Life

'Leonardo da Vinci was a Renaissance Man – a true polymath,' Edith read from her book. 'What does "polymath" mean, daddy?'

'It means someone who is good at lots of different subjects,' Frank said. 'There were quite a few people like that during the Renaissance, especially Leonardo da Vinci. And so a polymath came to be known as a "Renaissance Man".'

'Ah,' Edith scratched her nose. 'Is there such a thing as a Renaissance Woman?'

'There is these days,' I said. 'Or at least there should be, if feminism managed to achieve anything.'

'What's feminism?'

'Well, it's complicated. But basically it's the idea that women are as good as men.'

Edith looked at Alfie and Frank, then she smiled at me. 'Too right. We're not just as good as them. We're better than them.' She flicked the page and carried on reading. A few minutes later she looked up again.

'So is Vinci like an actual place?'

'Yup,' Frank said.

'Where is it?'

'It's got to be around here somewhere.' I took out our map of Italy and opened it up on the table. Edith scurried over to where I stood and peered over my shoulder.

'Here you go,' I pointed to a small dot on the map. 'It's just off the main road on the way into Florence. We're here and Vinci is there.'

'So it's close by,' Edith said. 'Can we go there? I'm really, really, really interested in Leonardo da Vinci. I've read so much about him. Remember that pop-up book you got me of his inventions? And the one I borrowed from school about his life? The one which describes how he built the horse statue, but the duke melted it down to make canons for a war? Please, please can we go to Vinci?'

She didn't need to sell the idea to me. This was what Road School was designed for. 'Of course we can.'

In school you have to learn the things that the teachers teach you, even if you don't find them all that interesting. Or, to be more accurate, you have to learn the things that the government wants your teachers to teach you, even if you don't really find them all that interesting. But Road School wasn't like that. Road School was about learning things *we* were interested in. So we went looking for Leonardo, and we found traces of his genius in all kinds of places. And the obvious place to begin was in Vinci, where he was born.

The road into Vinci didn't look promising. We drove down a long straight row of factories which were all shut tight. As we reached the outskirts of Vinci we realised why. It was market day and the centre of Vinci was jam-packed with locals and tourists who had come to buy food and crafts at the stalls. A long line of cars was backed up along the road through the town. Parking in the centre had been suspended for the market. Horns blared as drivers tried to back into tiny spaces. We headed through town and out the other side, looking all the time for somewhere to park. Eventually we found a space, a mile uphill from the Vinci museum. We parked up and headed down towards town, the kids trailing at our heels. Alfie moaned non-stop about the long walk. Edith was too excited to care. The moment had come when she finally got to commune with her hero.

The Museo Leonardiano di Vinci was housed inside the Palazzina Uzielli and the Conti Guidi Castle. It was small but perfectly formed. Inside there were recreations of Leonardo's famous drawings: a tank, a flying machine, mechanical clocks, a bicycle and a diving suit. Edith gazed in amazement at the different models. After we had finished our tour of the museum, we climbed up to the roof of the museum where you could look out across the beautiful rolling green hills towards Florence.

Edith turned to me with a smile on her face. 'Leonardo was a genius,' she said. 'He drew designs for all those models, hundreds of years before they were actually built. When I grow up I want to be an inventor, just like him.'

'I thought you said you wanted to be an artist,' Alfie said.

'Yes, that too.' Edith thought for a moment. 'And I'm going to be an accountant. And a basketball player. And an astronaut. Oh, and an ice cream connoisseur as well.'

Her brother looked sceptical. 'That's a lot of stuff to fit in.'

'Oh don't worry, Alfie. I'll manage it. Because I'm going to be a polymath, just like Leonardo da Vinci. Except that instead of being a Renaissance Man, I'll be a Renaissance Woman. Thanks to feminism.'

'Atta girl,' I said.

Crazy Horses

After visiting Vinci we had an afternoon to kill, so the plan was to visit Siena, a couple of hours' drive away. We wound our way through the rolling Tuscan countryside, parked up on the outskirts of town and headed downhill towards the centre. I only knew two things about Siena. First was that it gave its name to a colour of paint known as burnt sienna, which is a kind of browny-orange. According to my guidebook, the colour was originally produced in Siena during the Renaissance, by heating an earth pigment that contains iron oxide and manganese oxide. As we walked through the streets it was noticeable that all the houses were painted in the exact same burnt-orange colour. It was as if the name of the town had come to life in its architecture. The second thing I knew about Siena was that they held a very famous and very dangerous horse race twice each year called the Palio. We were going to have a look around the town and see where the crazy horses did their thing.

Eventually we made it through town and into the Piazza del Campo, the central square in Siena where the Palio di Siena takes place on 2 July and 16 August each year. The sides of the Campo were made up of thousands of thin brick pavers, sloping down towards the centre, which made it the perfect place to flop down and have a rest. The square was packed with tourists doing exactly that. First we headed into a nearby gelateria to buy the kids an ice cream each. This being Italy they had a lot of flavours to choose from. After five minutes of deliberation they made their choices: chocolate for Edith and caramel for Alfie. Then we went to sit among the crowds of people to eat the ice creams and admire the view.

'During the Palio, ten riders ride bareback three times around the Campo, wearing the colours of their city ward, on a dirt track laid especially for the purpose,' I read from my guidebook. 'The race is fast, and furious, and dangerous, as the riders often get thrown off their horses. But it is the horse who wins the race, not the rider.'

'So it doesn't really matter if the rider is still on the horse at the end of the race?' Edith said.

'Well, no. Except, presumably, to the riders if they have a painful landing.'

'Oww,' Alfie said.

I carried on reading. 'Thousands of spectators flock to the Campo to see the race, which usually lasts no more than ninety seconds. Tickets to see the event from a terrace in the square can cost upwards of 400 euros per person.'

Alfie licked his ice cream. 'That's crazy. Hundreds of euros to see a horse race that lasts less than two minutes.'

Edith did a quick calculation in her head. 'That's over four euros a second. You're right, Alfie. Totally crazy.'

'It is crazy,' Frank said. 'Crazy horses. I think we can all agree on that.'

'How much does an ice cream cost, daddy?' Edith licked the last bit of her ice cream and started to crunch her way down the cone.

'About three euros. And no, you can't have another one.'

Edith paused. She did another quick calculation: '400 euros could buy me 133 ice creams. I could try an awful lot of different flavours if I bought 133 of them. I think I'd rather have 133 ice creams than watch ninety seconds of crazy horses.'

'And I think you're a very wise girl,' Frank said.

Ring My Bell

Florence is stuffed full of Renaissance monuments, churches and buildings, as well as world renowned museums and art galleries. We had already explored the Cattedrale di Santa Maria del Fiore, and our next destination was the Uffizi Gallery, which hosted the artworks of famous Italian painters including Botticelli, Michelangelo and (of course) Leonardo da Vinci. But before that we were planning to climb Giotto's Campanile, probably the most famous of the bell towers in Florence.

Giotto's Campanile, or bell tower, stands in the Piazza del Duomo in the centre of Florence, right next to the Cathedral of Saint Mary of the Flowers. We stood looking up at the tower, which seemed to glow white in the late morning sunshine. It seemed like a very long way up to the top. A big sign outside the front door of the tower warned us that there were 414 steps to climb, and that we shouldn't attempt it unless we were sure we had sufficient levels of fitness. The sign said that it was not recommended for people with heart problems, vertigo or claustrophobia.

'That's a lot of stairs,' Alfie said.

'What's claustrophobia?' Edith wanted to know.

'It's a fear of getting stuck in a tight enclosed space,' Frank said.

Edith thought for a second. 'Is this going to be more PE?'

'That's the one,' I said.

Frank turned to me. 'Are you sure about doing this? I'm a big guy and I can get a bit freaked out in small spaces.'

'Come on you lot,' I said brightly. 'Stop worrying and moaning – it will be good exercise.'

We joined the queue that snaked back from the entrance and edged slowly forwards. When we arrived at the entrance we paid our entry fee, went through a barrier and stood behind a line of other tourists waiting to climb the stairs. Eventually we stepped into the enclosed space where the staircase began. Frank went first, followed by Alfie, then Edith, with me bringing up the rear. I could hear Edith counting each step under her breath as she climbed. The staircase was narrow and winding, and it had a very low roof. I could only see a little way in front of me because the staircase made a quarter turn every twelve stairs. Ahead of me, I could see Frank turning the corner, bent almost double, because that was the only way he could avoid hitting his head as he climbed.

There was barely room for two people to pass side by side. Unfortunately, as our batch of tourists climbed up the stairs, another batch was climbing down them. Where one person was larger than average, it was a very tight squeeze for two people to pass.

According to Edith's count, we were at step 204 when the line ground to a halt.

'What's going on?' I couldn't see around the corner where Frank and Alfie had just disappeared. I could, however, hear a heated conversation going on just ahead of me. Edith turned and sighed.

'Daddy seems to be wedged.'

Now this I had to see. I leaned over Edith's shoulder and peered around the corner. 'Ah, I see,' I said.

Frank was a large and irresistible force going upwards. Unfortunately, he had met the proverbial immovable object coming downwards, in the form of a hefty American. No matter which way he and Frank turned, there simply wasn't room for the two of them to pass each other. A logjam was building up behind the American coming down, just as it was behind me coming up. We had reached deadlock.

'Alfie,' I called up to him. 'You're going to have to push your father or we'll be stuck here all day.'

'That was *sooo* embarrassing,' Alfie muttered, as we stumbled up the last few steps and exited onto the roof. 'I can't believe I had to do that.'

It had been touch and go for a while, but with a bit of shoving of Frank from Alfie, and a bit of shoving of the American man from his wife, the two big guys had eventually squeezed past each other.

We stood admiring the view spread out in front of us, gazing at the domes and the towers and the terracotta rooftops of Florence. It was a stunningly beautiful sight. All of a sudden there was the sound of bells ringing from just below us. The entire tower seemed to vibrate beneath my feet. I looked at my watch. It was exactly midday.

'They're ringing the bells!' Edith shouted delightedly.

'Maybe they're doing it to celebrate the fact that I got daddy up here!' Alfie grinned at his dad.

'I just bloody well hope we can get him down again,' I said.

'Language, mummy!' Edith said. And then both of our children pealed with laughter, as the bells completed their midday chimes.

Message In a Bottle

Our family is not religious. In fact, we are so not religious that when the Jehovah's Witnesses knock on our door (which they do with alarming regularity) I can truthfully send them away with the words: 'Sorry but we're all atheists here.' Having said this, it would have been churlish to visit Rome and not go to see the Vatican City, especially since our hotel was close to the world famous home of the popes. As soon as we had unloaded our suitcases at the hotel on our arrival in Rome, we headed off down the road in the direction of the famous city state. The first challenge was trying to figure out how you actually got into the place. A high wall ran like an endless barrier on our right. We walked downhill, with the impenetrable wall to our right and the noisy Roman traffic to our left. Every few minutes, the kids would pipe up to ask how much further it was, and I would remind them that I didn't have a clue.

Finally, after a fifteen minute walk alongside the high wall, we found the street that led into Vatican City. Hundreds of people streamed around us, all going in the same direction, carrying colourful flags and dressed in clothing from around the world. There were old women in wheelchairs being pushed by frail looking elderly men. There were old men leaning on walking sticks, shuffling towards their destination at a snail's pace. It seemed like there were people here from all the far flung corners of the world.

Eventually we came out into the large open space of St Peter's Square, which was bordered on both sides by semi-circular colonnades. On top of each of the stone columns was the figure of a pope, martyr, evangelist or other religious figure.

'Who's that?' Edith said, pointing up to where a statue of a distinguished looking man balanced on top of one of the columns.

'Not a clue,' Frank said. 'Probably a pope.'

'Well, who's that one?'

'Dunno,' he said. 'Another pope?'

'You were a lot better at the German questions than you are at the Italian ones, daddy,' Edith said.

'It's very busy, isn't it?' I looked across the square. 'I wonder if there's something going on?' All around us, people were clapping and singing and generally celebrating. (When we got back to our hotel and checked online, we would discover that we had managed to time our visit to coincide with the canonisation mass for Pope John Paul II.)

'What a racket.' Alfie stuck his fingers in his ears.

'I'm glad we're not religious.' Edith did the same thing.

The children perched on some stone bollards and gave their father a quick quiz about popes and Catholicism and the Vatican. Luckily, having been brought up a Catholic before he lapsed into atheism, Frank knew at least some of the answers.

'And while we're here, you should send a postcard to your friends,' Frank said to the kids, as they slid down from the bollards and we prepared to head back to our hotel.

'Why?'

'Because the Vatican City operates its own postal service. And it issues its own special stamps.'

'And because your friends will be excited to know what you've been up to while they've been stuck at school doing months of SATs preparation.' It was about time these kids started to appreciate how lucky they were.

The children chose a postcard each and perched on the edge of a raised pavement to scribble their messages. They addressed the cards and stuck on the stamps.

'Where do we post them?' Edith said.

'Over there,' Frank pointed to a building with the words 'Poste Vaticane' emblazoned on its side in big yellow letters. The post office was closed, but there were two big yellow postboxes fixed to the wall outside.

'They will be so jealous when they get our messages!' Edith said, slipping her postcard into the postbox.

'We're so lucky not to be at school!' Alfie pushed his card into the postbox as well.

'Thank you!' Edith gave us both a hug. Alfie grudgingly did the same.

I smiled at Frank. 'Finally, a bit of gratitude!' And then we headed back to our hotel to get ready for tomorrow's big day out in Rome.

Hungry Like the Wolf

'How exciting is this?' I said to the kids, as we made our way through a huge stone archway and up on to the Palatine Hill. Even though it was still early in the day, it was already sweltering hot. The kids trudged up the hill after me, looking distinctly underwhelmed. Frank trailed at the rear. He was carrying a heavy backpack, weighed down with enough food and drink to get us through the day. The Palatine is the centremost of the seven hills of Rome, and one of the most ancient places in the city. We were here at the start of a full day exploring Rome. With time fast running out before our appointment with *The Last Supper*, we could only afford to spend two nights in Rome if we were going to have time to visit Naples and Sicily as well. That meant one day to do as many of the sights of Rome as we could. I had made a long list of top tourist destinations, and we were going to visit every one of them: the Palatine Hill, the Roman Forum, the Colosseum, the Pantheon, the Trevi Fountain and the Spanish Steps.

The Palatine Hill was flush with archaeology – all around us there were buildings in the process of excavation. The hillside was littered with stone columns and dotted with the residences of Roman emperors. There were ancient tunnels and museums full of mosaics and Roman pottery. But as well as all this, the Palatine Hill was special because, according to Roman mythology, it was the location of the Lupercal. This was cave where (so the legend says) Romulus and his brother Remus were raised by the she-wolf Lupa. Later on, Romulus would kill his brother and go on to found the city of Rome. The children listened, enthralled, as I told them about the legend of the wolf and the mythology of how Rome was founded.

'I'm as thirsty as a drain and as hungry as a wolf,' Edith announced after an hour and a half of traipsing around the sights of the Palatine. The sun was high in the sky now, and we were hot, sweaty and tired. We collapsed onto a couple of wooden benches in the shade of some cypress trees. Two mangy looking pigeons pecked at the dirt on the ground in front of us.

'I'm starving too,' Alfie said.

Frank passed me the backpack and I fished inside. 'You can start by eating these,' I passed Edith and Alfie a foil package each, containing squashed cheese sandwiches.

'Can't I have some crisps first?' Edith said.

'No. Eat your sandwiches. Then you can have some crisps.'

Edith opened the foil and immediately dropped the entire round of sandwiches onto the ground.

'Whoops.' She looked up at me and smiled.

'Well done.' I wasn't totally convinced that it had been an accident. 'Pick them up then, as quick as you can. We might be able to salvage them if we apply the five second rule.'

As Edith bent down to retrieve her now dusty sandwiches, a flock of half-starved pigeons swooped down and landed in front of her. They started pecking at her lunch, making loud squabbling noises as they tried to stake their claim to a morsel of food.

Edith looked at the pigeons in disgust. 'Well, I can't eat my sandwiches now,' she pointed out. 'Those birds are riddled with disease. What is it you always call them, mummy?'

'Rats with wings,' I said.

'Can I have some crisps instead?' I sighed loudly, fished a packet of ready salted crisps out of the backpack and handed them to her.

'Whoops,' Alfie said, tipping his uneaten sandwiches onto the ground in front of him. Half the pigeons immediately turned their attentions to our son's lunch. The squabbling noise rose in volume as more and more pigeons joined the hungry mob. I sighed again and handed Alfie a packet of crisps as well.

'It's funny how they never seem to drop their crisps, isn't it, Frank?' Frank nodded and made a harrumphing sound.

'Talking of lunch …' He had a hopeful note in his voice.

'Don't you start,' I zipped up the backpack. 'Right everybody, let's go. We've got a lot of sights to fit in today. Next stop the Roman Forum.'

We Are Family

'I need a wee!' Edith hopped from one foot to another.

We were standing on the edge of the roundabout at the Piazza Venezia in the centre of Rome. We had toured the ancient wonders of the Roman Forum and marvelled at the historic majesty of the Colosseum. Now we were on our way to the Pantheon, which was still the world's largest unreinforced dome, 2,000 years after it was first built. Traffic whizzed round the roundabout in front of us. Horns blared. Drivers swore out of open windows. A policeman was trying to stop the traffic so that he could direct pedestrians across the road. The Italian drivers were completely ignoring his commands.

'I'm desperate for the loo,' Edith jiggled on the spot as we waited for a gap in the traffic.

'You're just going to have to wait until we find a toilet,' I said. 'I haven't exactly seen lots of public loos in this city.'

'Why don't we go into a cafe and have a drink?' Frank suggested. 'I don't know about anyone else, but I'm thirsty *and* I'm starving. Then you can have a wee in the cafe.'

'Great idea!' Edith said.

'I'm hungry too,' Alfie said.

'Going to a cafe in the centre of Rome is like going to a cafe in Oxford Street,' I pointed out. 'We are going to get completely ripped off. That's why we brought a packed lunch with us, remember? Not so that you could feed it to a flock of Roman pigeons.'

'Hey! Check that out!' Frank said, gesturing across the roundabout. I don't think I had ever heard Frank so excited, even when he wrote that really clever spreadsheet to calculate the cost of the family's Christmas presents.

'What is it?' I peered into the distance.

'Wow!' Edith had spotted it too, whatever it was.

'O … M … G.' Now Alfie had spotted it as well.

'What?' I said. 'What is it that you've all seen but I haven't?'

'The Caffé Castellino,' Frank pointed to a cafe on the other side of the roundabout.

'This is like fate,' Edith said. 'A cafe with our name on it, just at the moment when I desperately need a toilet.'

Given that my surname is Cowley, it's probably best to explain at this point that I don't share a surname with the children, or with Frank either. Frank's surname is, as you will have gathered by now, Castellino. But because we're not married, I am not Mrs Castellino. When we had kids we decided to go with Frank's surname rather than mine, mainly on the basis that it is a lot more attractive than Cowley. This causes no end of confusion when cold callers phone up and say, 'Is that Mrs Castellino?' and I say, 'No.' It also leads to perplexity at passport control when I travel alone with the children. We've occasionally discussed marriage over the twenty-five years we've been together, but the idea of doing it 'for tax purposes', as Frank once suggested, does not exactly make me feel warm, fuzzy and romantic.

We waited for a break in the traffic and then we ran at top speed across the roundabout, narrowly avoiding being mown down by a crazy Italian taxi driver. Edith hurried into the Caffé Castellino, Frank and Alfie close behind her. I followed reluctantly after them.

'Can I just check the prices before we get too settled?' I said. But it was too late. A waiter was already showing Frank and the children to a table. He tossed a couple of menus in our direction.

'Where's the toilet?' Edith wriggled and jiggled.

'We're not paying these kinds of prices,' I handed Frank the menu in disgust. 'It's six euros for a coffee and eight euros for an ice cream. What a rip-off!'

'Where's the toilet?' Edith said again.

'It doesn't look like we have much choice,' Frank pointed out. 'It's either that, or our daughter will have to trail around in urine soaked clothes all afternoon.'

'Come with me.' I grabbed Edith's hand. 'And you lot, don't order anything until I get back.' Alfie and Frank were both studying the menu and licking their lips.

I found the toilets which were located towards the back of the cafe. I stood outside, waiting for Edith to finish. From inside, I heard a sigh of relief, followed by a sound like a waterfall. The sound seemed to go on for several minutes. Finally we shuffled back to the table where Frank was still studying the menu.

'They're a bit slow in here,' Frank said. 'He still hasn't taken our order yet.' The waiter was nowhere to be seen.

'Then let's do a runner.' I headed for the exit, pulling Edith along behind me. Alfie followed close on my heels, with Frank following.

'I knew we'd do a lot of fascinating things on this trip,' Frank said, when we were safely outside. 'But I didn't imagine I would find myself doing a runner from the Caffè Castellino.' I lined the three of them up underneath the cafe sign that bore their name. Then I snapped three quick pictures of the Castellino family, and we dashed off in the direction of the Pantheon.

Money

After a day spent stumbling around the hot, overcrowded, historic wonders of Rome, it was time to visit the Trevi Fountain. I had a quick check on the map and figured out which street we needed to take. But in the end it wasn't difficult to find. All we had to do was to allow the crowd to pull us along the narrow, dusty streets that led from the Pantheon towards our destination. It was as though the fountain was magnetic, and the tourists were being drawn towards it by the lure of its cooling water.

As we turned the corner and the fountain came into view, the children gasped in amazement. The Trevi Fountain is a rococo marvel, with Tritons and horses over naturalistic rocky formations. It was completed in 1762, although it looked weirdly modern after a morning of staring at ancient Roman columns.

'Wow!' Edith said.

'Cool!' Alfie said.

The children hurried through the crowds and down some steps to the edge of the water. There were hundreds of tourists gathered around the fountain. Despite the crush, the air felt cool and refreshing. The water made a roaring sound as it gushed out of the fountain and crashed into the pool.

'There's a story about the fountain,' I told the kids as we joined them, perching on the lip of the pool. 'The story goes that if you throw a coin into the Trevi Fountain, then one day you will return to Rome. You're meant to throw it over your shoulder, backwards, though.'

'I'd love to come back. Give me a euro.' I handed Edith a one euro coin. She wriggled around until her back was facing the fountain, then she lobbed the coin high over her shoulder and it splashed into the water.

'Give me one too.' I handed a coin to Alfie and he did the same thing.

'Apparently around two to three thousand euros are thrown into the fountain each day,' I said.

'Wow!' Alfie looked at the piles of coins sparkling under the water in the afternoon sunshine. 'That's a lot of money.'

'That's a lot of people coming back to Rome,' Edith said. 'Maybe that's why it's so busy.'

'Ah, but there's another story about the fountain,' Frank said. 'A much more interesting one.'

'What's that then?' We all wanted to know.

'Apparently, they found out that a man was taking the coins from the fountain. His nickname was D'Artagnan. He would turn up with two accomplices and a broom, then he would sweep the coins into piles and take them away with him.'

'But that's stealing, daddy!' Edith looked horrified. She glanced back at the fountain where her euro sat among the piles of other coins, glistening in the sun.

'Well you'd certainly think so, wouldn't you?' Frank was enjoying the chance to tell us his story. 'But when D'Artagnan was arrested for stealing, a judge decided he couldn't be a thief.'

'Why not?'

'Well, because the coins had been discarded, it wasn't stealing to take them. Plus they found out that the local police were watching, but they didn't intervene to stop him.'

'But that's just plain wrong!' Edith looked really cross at the idea of the police standing by while someone scooped up her money and made off with it. She scratched her chin. 'Well, he's not having my euro. I didn't discard it for some thief to have it. I'm going to take it back.'

'Me too!' Alfie said.

The kids reached into the water, fished around a bit and scooped out a euro coin each. There was a policeman on duty close by. He looked over at us suspiciously.

'Ah, but now that you've taken your coin out, you won't get to return to Rome,' I pointed out.

'Daddy, have you got a one cent coin?' Edith said. 'I'm not wasting a whole euro on D'Artagnan.'

'That's my girl.' Frank handed each of the kids a one cent coin, they both turned their backs on the fountain again and tossed the coins over their shoulders.

'Now I'm definitely coming back to Rome!' Edith said. 'But next time I'm going to spend longer than one day here.'

Then we gathered up our bags, left the cooling environs of the beautiful Trevi Fountain and headed off to be totally underwhelmed by the Spanish Steps.

Blue Hotel

'I thought you said the hotel was close to Pompeii?' Frank moaned, as we passed yet another sign that told us the archaeological site of Pompeii was in the opposite direction. We had been driving up and down the busy, litter strewn roads of the area around Pompeii for almost an hour now. Our hotel was proving illusive. The satnav told us that the address we had for the hotel didn't even exist, so we had resorted to a good old-fashioned map.

'Are we going to be there soon?' Edith piped up from the back seat. 'I'm starving.'

'Me too,' Alfie said.

'You've only mentioned that about a million times already.' I tried desperately to make sense of the map.

'I'm sure we'll find it soon,' Frank made another U-turn and headed back down the road in the opposite direction.

'Look! That's it over there!' The hotel sign was cleverly hidden behind a tall palm tree planted just in front of it. Frank swerved into the car park, pulled into a parking space and turned off the engine. We got out of the car and stretched our aching legs.

'I thought you said that this place had a view of Vesuvius?' Frank said.

'That's what it said on the listing.' I pointed through the rapidly darkening sky to where you could just see the tip of a black shape in the far distance. The shape was covered in cloud. 'Maybe that's it.'

'That's only a view of Vesuvius if our room is on the roof,' Frank said, unhelpfully.

As we stumbled in through the hotel entrance, trailing dirty suitcases and starving children behind us, the man on reception glowered at us and then grunted in Italian. After I'd shown him a print-out of my booking, and we'd done a brief exchange of hand signals, we were given a key and a Wi-Fi code. We headed up a flight of stairs to our room.

'What does this sign even mean?' Frank pointed to a little plaque outside the room. He read it out: "NESSUN CIBO NELLE CAMERE".'

'No idea. Why don't you Google it?'

Frank unlocked the door, flopped onto the bed and flipped open his laptop. Then he tapped away at the keys. 'It means "No food in the rooms". Great. It's 8 o'clock. We're all starving. We're not allowed to eat in the room, so we'll have to have dinner in the over-priced hotel restaurant.'

'No we won't.'

'But I'm starving, mum,' Alfie said.

'Me too,' Edith added.

I got up, grabbed my handbag and headed for the door.

'Hey,' Frank said. 'Where are you going?'

'It said on TripAdvisor that there's a great barbeque chicken place just up the road from the hotel. I'll go and buy us some food there, and we can eat it on the balcony. Surely they won't mind if we do that.'

'Weren't you just telling me how TripAdvisor ...' I didn't wait around to hear Frank finish his sentence. I was on a mission to feed my family.

I left the hotel and trudged up the poorly lit main road in the dusky twilight. Half the shops were permanently shut, their windows boarded up or covered in heavy-duty metal shutters. I passed a patch of waste ground. It was scattered with discarded rubbish and used needles. Cars raced past me on the main road, spewing fumes into the hot night air. As I picked my way along the uneven pavement, packs of stray dogs gnawed at the chicken bones that littered my path. I tripped over a broken paving slab and trod in a dog turd.

'Damn!' I wiped my shoe on the edge of the pavement to try to remove the sticky brown mess. A disgusting smell wafted up to my nostrils.

Eventually I reached what I felt had to be the 'great barbeque chicken place'. It consisted of a large metal barbeque on the street with lots of mangy looking cats hanging around it. The chicken vendor was throwing pieces of toxic looking wood into the fire and grilling some of the skinniest chickens I had ever seen.

I pointed. The chicken vendor mumbled. After a long wait, during which time the scrawny cats sniffed around my ankles, I was rewarded with chicken and chips for my family. The chicken vendor chucked our dinner into a carrier bag and handed it over. I passed him a bunch of crushed euro notes.

As I entered the hotel with the carrier bag, the manager gave me a suspicious look and sniffed the air. I smiled my sweetest smile, hid the carrier bag behind my back and scurried over to the stairs. I knocked on the door to our room and Frank opened it. I slipped out of my shoes and dumped them outside the door. I didn't want to stink out the room with dog poo.

'The hunter-gatherer returns with dinner,' I said. 'Quick. Let's get it out on the balcony before they catch us with food in the room.'

I carried the bag out to the balcony and dished out the trays of food. 'Doesn't it look delicious? Dive in everyone!'

'Mmm, this is great, mum,' Alfie chewed on a chicken leg. 'Thank you.'

'Thanks for this fantastic dinner,' Edith scooped chips into her mouth like there was no tomorrow.

'Are you sure this is chicken?' Frank picked up a bone and nibbled it doubtfully. Luckily, it was too dark to tell.

Ain't No Mountain High Enough

The drive up Vesuvius was simultaneously breathtaking and heart-stopping. Ahead of us, the volcano glowered, a towering black presence in the sky. Behind us, the Bay of Naples spread out, shimmering blue in the sun. In the far distance were a handful of islands – Capri, Ischia and Procida. There was a scattering of clouds in the azure sky. The road up to the top of Vesuvius was narrow, rutted and winding. It was full of crazy Italian drivers and huge tourist coaches. Frank seemed to have taken inspiration for his driving style from *Top Gear* and was rounding each bend at top speed. I felt sure an oncoming coach would eventually force us off the road.

As we neared the summit, we came across a policeman blocking the road. He signalled to us that we should turn around, explaining in broken English that there were no parking spaces left at the top, and that we had to park on the road down here. A minibus would take us to the top.

'We can get the bus to the top and back down,' Frank said. 'Then we won't have to walk too much.'

'Great idea!' The kids let out a chorus of approval at Frank's idea.

'Let's see how much it costs.' I wasn't too sure that Frank's idea made sense. After all, how long could the walk to the top be from this point?

We approached the minibus and made enquiries. The driver told us that it would cost us five euros to get up and back down. Each.

'That's twenty euros, Frank. It's a total con. We should walk. Then the children can spend the money on souvenirs instead. I bet it's just around that corner.' I pointed ahead of us, where the road bent around to the right. We could see the summit of Vesuvius in the near distance. It didn't seem to be too far away.

'I bet it isn't just around that corner,' Frank said. 'It's very hot today. We should take the bus. Really.'

'No. We should definitely walk. Think of it as more PE.' I smirked at him.

'Well, I reserve the right to say "I told you so" if this all goes wrong,' Frank smirked back at me. He still hadn't forgotten my reaction to the 'bloody petrol incident'.

As we began to trudge our way up the road to the summit, Frank dashed off ahead and was soon out of sight. I trailed behind him, with the kids in my wake. It was hot. Very hot.

'I'm tired,' Edith said. 'Is it much further?'

'We've only just started. You can't be tired yet,' I said. 'Anyway, I'm sure it's just around that bend. Keep going. It'll be worth it once we get to the top.'

'I'm tired too.' Alfie joined in the litany of complaints as we rounded the first bend and it became clear that the summit hadn't been 'just around that bend'. 'Is it much further?'

'You've only been walking for ten minutes. Come on. It'll be worth it once we get to the top.' A minibus full of tourists drove past us. The kids looked longingly in its direction.

'I'm tired,' Edith said, ten minutes later, as we rounded yet another bend and it became clear that the summit wasn't going to be around any bend anytime soon. 'Are we nearly there yet, mum?'

'I'm totally sure it's around the next bend. And when we get there you can spend the twenty euros we saved on buying stuff.'

'Ice creams?' The kids wanted to know.

'Sure.'

An hour later, we reached the ticket office at the foot of the volcano. We were hot, tired and very sweaty. By this point I was carrying Edith on my back and dragging Alfie up behind me. A dark and angry looking cloud shrouded the summit of Vesuvius. There was a big sign by the ticket office saying 'No refunds if the view at the top is obscured by cloud'.

'What kept you?' Frank said. 'See how the clouds have come down already?'

'It was a bit of a distance.'

'I told you so. We really should have caught that minibus.'

'Can we have our twenty euros worth of ice cream now?' Edith slid off my back.

'What twenty euros worth of ice cream?' Frank looked at me with a grimace.

'Don't forget, daddy,' Edith said, as I handed her the money. 'I'm in training to be an ice cream connoisseur. And I've still got a lot of flavours to try.' She grabbed her brother's hand and dragged him towards the nearest ice cream van with a massive smile on her face.

Walking On Sunshine

After another half an hour of climbing, this time up the crumbling black igneous rock that coated the sides of the crater wall, we finally made it to the top of Vesuvius. The climb was steep and hard going; the black volcanic rocks shifted under our feet, dust rising into the air in a choking cloud. This was turning out to be a day of full-on physical activity. As we reached the summit, and rounded the final bend, we got our first view into the crater. Puffs of steam drifted gently out of the bowl and the smell of sulphur hung in the air. A heavy rain cloud completed the scene.

'Great weather to see the view,' Frank said. The volcano was completely shrouded in cloud and the Bay of Naples had disappeared.

'Where's the molten lava? Where's the fire? And why does this place smell so bad?' There was a note of bitter disappointment in Edith's voice. 'It's not a volcano if there isn't red hot lava spewing out of it! We came all this way for nothing!' She began to sob.

'It *is* a volcano,' Alfie said. (He's the family expert on volcanoes. He has read an awful lot of books on them.) 'Technically Vesuvius is a stratovolcano. A stratovolcano has both violent eruptions and pyroclastic flows.'

'What's a pyroclastic flow?' Edith said.

'That's like what happened at Pompeii and Herculaneum,' he said. 'The volcano erupts really violently and you get a massive cloud of smoke and ash that covers the land and chokes everyone to death. No human being can outrun a pyroclastic flow. It means certain death. Vesuvius is quiet now. But it could erupt at any moment. *Bang!*' Edith jumped in to the air. She began to weep even more loudly.

'I'm scared,' she howled, 'I want to go back to the hotel.'

'At least let's take a look around first,' Frank said, 'seeing as we walked all this way.'

We moved off around the rim of the crater, passing stall after stall selling souvenirs and postcards. Most of the stalls were offering snow globes which seemed rather incongruous in the hot, steamy surroundings of a volcano. And there were, of course, lots of boxes of volcanic rocks.

'Look Alfie!' Edith leaned over a stall to examine something with a note of wonder in her voice.

'What?' Alfie hurried over to where his sister was standing. 'OMG,' he said, as he saw what she was looking at.

'Alfie … it's … it's … obsidian.' Edith's eyes were wide and shining.

'Wow,' Alfie paused for a moment in wonder. 'Obsidian. Amazing.'

'How on earth do they know that the shiny black stuff is obsidian?' Frank asked me. 'And why are they getting so excited about it? Did they get into geology without me realising?'

'*Minecraft*. They mine obsidian on that, apparently.'

'So they did learn something from all that time in front of a screen.'

'Daddy, daddy,' Edith was jiggling with excitement, all fear of the volcano forgotten. 'Please can we buy some rocks?'

'You just spent twenty euros on ice cream.'

'Please, please, please can we buy some rocks?' Alfie ran over to join us. Frank handed them ten euros each, and they dashed eagerly back to the stall.

We carried on walking around the crater, the children cradling boxes of rocks in their hands as though they contained important treasure and not just a selection of igneous rocks and minerals.

'This is sulphur, and this is quartz, and this is pyrite,' Alfie told his sister, picking out each of the rocks and minerals in turn and explaining all about them.

'It looks like there's gold in it!' Edith exclaimed.

'They call it fool's gold. It's not really gold, but it looks a bit like it.'

Halfway around the crater of Vesuvius there was a viewpoint where we could stand and look down on the Bay of Naples and its surroundings. Or rather, where we could have stood and looked down on the Bay of Naples and its surroundings if they hadn't been completely obscured by cloud. I cursed myself under my breath for insisting that we should not take the minibus to the top.

And then, just as we were about to give up on the weather, the heavy cloud that had been sitting on the volcano moved inland and the scenery was suddenly revealed. The view was stunning. The land stretched off towards the far horizon where it met the mountains of the Sorrento Peninsula. Verdant green vegetation spread down the cone of the volcano, where the land had become fertile through centuries of volcanic activity. The Bay of Naples glimmered in the afternoon sunshine. Spectacular islands rose out of the deep blue water. Huge puffs of white cloud drifted up from the valley, before skimming the top of Vesuvius and passing inland. The sun felt warm and soothing on my face.

'Wow.' Frank turned to me and smiled. 'This was definitely worth the walk.'

'Being here is a *lot* better than getting here,' I said. I leaned over and gave Frank a big sloppy kiss.

'Yuk!' Alfie and Edith both looked at us in disgust. Then they ran off laughing into the distance to carry on exploring the crater.

Ashes to Ashes

The Internet had promised us that our hotel was 'close to' Pompeii. Unsurprisingly, in yet another Internet fail, the reality proved to be rather different. We ended up driving several miles to the famous town that had been buried by a cloud of pyroclastic ash in AD 79. Given how famous it is as a tourist attraction, Pompeii was surprisingly quiet at this time of year. We paid our entrance fee and headed into the maze of streets. Everywhere we looked there were strange buildings full of beautiful mosaics.

The most famous sight in Pompeii surely has to be the casts of the people who were buried in the volcanic eruption. According to my guidebook, the casts were made in the most ingenious manner, by pouring plaster into the hollow spaces that were left behind when the bodies rotted away. Once the lava was chipped away from the plaster, the shapes were revealed. The positions in which the bodies lay gave a true sense of the fear that the people must have felt. There was a woman leaning over her child to protect him from the deluge of pyroclastic ash.

'It's very sad,' Edith said.

'You're not going to cry again, are you, mum?' Alfie looked at me uncertainly.

'No, I'm not.'

The guides we had picked up on our arrival at Pompeii told us that one of the highlights of a visit was the famous mosaic of a dog in the House of the Tragic Poet. After wandering the streets for what felt like hours, we finally found the house. We hunted around inside, looking for a dog mosaic.

'Here it is!' Alfie rushed over and bent down to look at it. We joined him. The image was constructed of black and pale brown tiles. It showed a dog on a chain. The dog seemed to be growling at us from inside the ancient image.

'Cave Canem.' Edith read out the letters at the bottom of the mosaic. 'What does it mean?' We all looked to Frank for an answer. He had done Latin at his boarding school. It wasn't on the curriculum at my inner London comprehensive.

Frank laughed. 'See if you can figure it out.'

'Well, canine is to do with dogs, so I guess "canem" means dog,' Alfie said, looking to his dad to check whether he was right. Frank nodded.

'Put the dog in a cave?' Edith suggested.

'Nope,' Frank said.

'Ah, I've got it!' I said. 'It's like a doormat with a warning sign.'

Both the kids jumped up and down in frustration. 'Tell us! Tell us!' they insisted.

Frank and I spoke simultaneously: 'Beware of the dog!'

Our plan for the following day was to visit Pompeii's twin city of Herculaneum, which was also swamped by pyroclastic surges from the eruption in AD 79. While Pompeii was inland, Herculaneum was on the coast, and this meant that some of the inhabitants managed to escape via the sea.

As we drove through the narrow streets towards Herculaneum, we could tell that it was going to be busy. After driving round and round in circles for half an hour, we finally managed to grab ourselves a parking space. Cleverly, we had managed to time our trip to coincide with a 'free entry to all monuments' day, funded by the Italian government. On the plus side, entry was free; on the downside, the place was rammed. The queue for free tickets stretched around the side of the building and out into the hot sun. I slumped down to wait with the kids in a shady spot on the grass while Frank queued up for the tickets.

The strangest thing about Herculaneum is that it is basically underground. Logically, this makes sense. The town was swamped by the pyroclastic surge from Vesuvius, and so to excavate it the Italians had to dig it out from underneath the volcanic mud. Because the excavations didn't start until 1738, and then ceased once the nearby town of Pompeii was discovered, the modern day town around the ancient site grew up at what was now ground level. As we walked towards the entrance, along with a huge crowd of visitors, I peered over a wall and into the ancient city far below us. It gave me the strangest sensation of looking down and into the distant past.

'Woah,' Alfie sounded more excited than I had heard him in a while.

'What is it?'

He pointed. 'Skeletons. Down there. That is so cool.' It seemed like a lifetime ago that our son had last seen a skeleton, in the underground caves of the Harz. This time, though, it wasn't a single skeleton of a bear, it was lots of skeletons of ancient human beings.

We all stopped and stared over the wall. Below us was a row of small buildings with curved roofs. The skeletons were lying inside them. I checked my guidebook to see what it was all about.

'Apparently, that bit was the beach and the coastline in ancient times. And those were the boat houses. The skeletons belong to the people who were waiting on the shore for rescue to come from the sea.'

'That's very sad,' Edith said. 'But I still don't get it. The beach is all the way over there.' She pointed to our left, where we could see the sea off in the distance.

'Ah! I see.' Alfie nodded his head sagely. 'The pyroclastic flow from Vesuvius would have poured down over the town and into the sea, burying the city and creating a new piece of land on top of it. So when they rebuilt the city later on, it was at a different level, and the coast was further out to sea.'

As we wandered around the hot, busy streets of Herculaneum that afternoon, I found myself thinking about school, and about how our children could have learned all this stuff in the classroom or even just from a book. I thought about the past, buried under volcanic ash for centuries, finally brought back into the light of day. I thought about how we had been here, and seen the modern day outcome of something that happened almost 2,000 years ago. And I felt certain that, when it comes to learning, nothing quite beats doing it in real life.

I Am the Mob

After an epic journey down Italy, and a quick boat trip across the Straits of Messina, we had finally arrived in Sicily. We were settled into our new apartment, and we were ready for our first full day of Sicilian sightseeing.

'I'm starving,' Frank said. 'I want lunch now. I'm not going to do any tourist stuff until I've had some lunch. Before we came on this trip you promised me that I could follow my interests. And today I am interested in having a delicious and epic lunch.'

We drove along the sea road, heading south towards Taormina on the east coast of the island. There were plenty of supermarkets lining the road but all the restaurants looked closed.

'How about this place?' I pulled over to the side of the road. We had just passed a restaurant decorated with sea designs on the outside. The name of the restaurant was written on the front in a deep red colour: Trattoria di Taormina. We jumped out of the car and wandered back up the road to take a look.

'I'm starving,' Alfie said.

'Me too,' said Edith. 'Do you think they do steak?'

'I'm guessing from the painting on the front that this is a fish restaurant,' I warned Edith.

'Yuk!' Edith does not do well with fish.

'It looks good, but they don't take credit cards.' Frank was reading the menu that was tacked up on the wall outside the restaurant. 'Have you got any cash?'

'Fifty euros.'

'Surely that'll be enough? Sicily is cheap. And we can just pick the cheapest things on the menu.'

As we stood there procrastinating about whether or not this was a good choice of venue to find Frank his epic lunch, the manager of the restaurant poked his head out of the door.

'You hungry.' He spoke with a heavy Sicilian accent. It sounded more like a statement of fact than a question. He wasn't wrong.

'We're starving,' Alfie confirmed.

'Famished,' Edith added.

'Then you come in. We feed you!' He held his arms open in a gesture of welcome.

'I've only got fifty euros,' Frank warned him.

'No problem!' the manager said. 'You pay what you think the food is worth.'

'I'm not sure,' I said, but since everyone else had already trooped inside I had no option but to follow. Inside the restaurant there were only a couple of other customers eating small dishes of what looked like Sicilian tapas. The smell was delicious. We settled down at a table and the manager handed us a menu. There were no prices on it.

'This looks a bit fancy,' I said to Frank. 'And there are no prices.' It seemed to be some kind of tasting menu. Every single item on the menu was a fish dish of some kind. There were seven different kinds of prawn, there was fish in red pepper sauce, octopus three different ways, spaghetti with squid ink. But not a steak in sight.

'No steak?' Edith sounded horrified. Frank called the waiter over and explained the problem.

'I send my wife to supermarket. She buy steak there.' A few minutes later a small, well-padded woman hurried out of the kitchen and off through the front door of the restaurant.

Dish after dish of delicious food was brought to the table. Edith ate her steak. The rest of us filled our faces with fantastic Sicilian fish. Eventually we could eat no more. Frank leaned back in his chair, placed his hands on his stomach and heaved a contented sigh. Then he poked out his tongue.

'Is it black?' he said. It was, from the squid ink spaghetti.

'That looks disgusting, Frank,' I said. 'Don't even try to kiss me until that wears off.'

'You've got to take a photo of that, mum,' Alfie said.

Eventually the manager came over and cleared the final set of plates.

'How much does it come to, then?' Frank said.

'I say, you pay what you think the food is worth,' the manager headed off to speak to his wife, who had poked her head out from the kitchen.

'Thirty euros?' I suggested.

'That seems a bit mean. They did go out and buy steak especially for Edith. And we should probably bear in mind that Sicily is the home of the Mafia.'

'What's the Mafia?' Edith spoke a little too loudly for my liking. An elderly gentleman who had been sitting a few tables away from us, all the time we were eating, looked up and over in our direction. His eyes narrowed and he frowned. I gulped.

'Pay him the full fifty euros,' I told Frank. 'Better safe than sorry.'

The manager came back to our table and handed Frank a slip of paper. 'I write you the bill. For sixty euros.'

'But I told you I only have fifty euros,' Frank pointed out.

'You come back tomorrow. You bring me another ten.'

'He was very trusting,' Alfie said as we got into the car and drove off in the direction of Taormina.

'I don't think trust has got much to do with it,' I said. 'We'd better come back with ten euros tomorrow. Unless you want your dad to wake up with a horse's head in his bed.'

La Isla Bonita

As we drove along the coast road past Taormina, on our way back from a visit to Syracuse, a wide bay opened up before us. In the middle of the bay was a tiny island set in a sparkling blue sea. Shards of light glittered on the water. People strolled and relaxed on the beach in the warm afternoon sunshine.

'Wow, look at that!' Edith said.

'Can we go there?' Alfie wanted to know.

'It does look gorgeous, doesn't it?' I smiled at Frank. 'And I did pack the swimsuits and towels, just in case.'

Frank turned into a parking area and pulled up. We piled out of the car and grabbed our towels from the boot. Then we trooped over the road, down a set of steps and onto the beach. The beach was pebbly, but the scene was stunning. The shore swept around in an arc to a central point. To get to the island you had to walk across some stepping stones that were submerged beneath an azure sea. We settled down on the pebbles and took off our sandals.

'I'm heading over to the island with the kids,' I said.

'I'll wait here to keep an eye on our stuff.' Frank lay back on a towel, closed his eyes and began to snore.

When we got back from our visit to the island, Frank was looking rather flustered. He wiped some beads of sweat from his forehead.

'I feel like I've been assaulted,' he said.

'Poor daddy!' Edith hurried over to give him a hug.

'I think I'll just about survive.'

'What happened?' I said.

'Well, there were these Thai women. They kept offering me a foot massage.' Frank gestured to a spot further up the beach where a group of exotic looking women were moving from tourist to tourist.

'And? Why didn't you just say no?'

'I did. I kept saying no, but they didn't want to take no for an answer.'

'I can give you a foot massage later, if you want.' I smiled at

Frank. Our latest accommodation was a spacious top floor flat with a large roof terrace and separate bedrooms for us and the kids.

'That'd be nice,' Frank had a big grin plastered across his face. 'Oh, and by the way, it didn't look like a foot massage was all that they were offering.'

'Why? What else were they offering?' Edith said.

Frank winked at me. 'I'm not sure. But I think I might be able to figure it out tonight, with the help of your mother.'

Road to Nowhere

After a glorious few days in Sicily, it was time to head back up the length of Italy and get to Milan for our long awaited appointment with Leonardo's *Last Supper*. Rather than driving back up Italy, putting our tyres at risk on the rutted Italian motorways, Frank had done the maths, created a spreadsheet and decided that it was more cost effective for us to head back in the relative comfort of a ship's cabin. Our ferry to Genoa was due to leave mid-afternoon, which meant that there was plenty of time for us to check out of our apartment, visit Mount Etna and then drive north-west towards Sicily's capital city, Palermo, where we would embark. The ferry company we were going to travel with was called 'Grandi Navi Veloci'. The kids were very amused when Frank told them that this translated as 'Big Fast Boat'.

The summit of Mount Etna was hidden in the clouds, as it had been since we had arrived in Sicily. Unlike Vesuvius, which was a fairly neat, tidy volcano, Etna sprawled across the surrounding land like a fat dollop of lava. According to the volcano book we had with us, Etna was originally in the sea, just off the island of Sicily. Over the centuries a series of volcanic eruptions had filled in the sea around Etna, until it had become part of the island itself. I plugged our destination into the satnav and we set off. The road up to the volcano was winding and badly signposted, but it didn't take us too long to reach the car park near the top. We had a good look around and the children gasped in wonder at postcards featuring images of the most recent eruption, when the buildings that surrounded the car park had been set on fire by a lava flow.

'We'd better head off now,' Frank said. 'Our ferry leaves in four hours, and I'm not sure how long it'll take us to get over to Palermo.'

We got back in the car and I plugged the address in Palermo into the satnav.

'Don't worry,' I said, 'it's only a couple of hours from here to there.'

We had a road map of Sicily, but the sides of Mount Etna were crisscrossed by what looked like hundreds of tiny lanes. If the way up had been a bit confusing, the route down looked incomprehensible. There was a dual carriageway once we got down off the volcano, but it was impossible to figure out the best way to get to it. I spread open the map and conferred with Frank.

'Shall we just trust the satnav? It's probably going to be better than trusting me to read this map.'

'Famous last words,' Frank said. 'Surely you've heard all those stories about people relying on their satnav and ending up stuck in a river?'

'Well, I can drive and you can navigate if you want.' I shoved the map towards him.

Frank started up the engine. 'We'll trust the satnav. It'll be fine.'

The satnav directed us down the south side of Mount Etna, along a series of tiny, winding tracks, surrounded by fields of black lava which stretched as far as the eye could see. From time to time the road surface would turn to a gritty volcanic dust and I would start to panic, but the satnav seemed to know where it was taking us. We were in the hands of technology now. We had no option but to trust it. The sides of the road were scattered with the burnt-out remains of houses, some of them half buried under the lava flow. After half an hour, we were finally approaching the foot of the volcano. In the distance we could see the dual carriageway to Palermo. It cut its way along the bottom of a verdant valley. Cars moved along it at high speed.

'Surely we must join the main road soon?' Frank said. The satnav directed us to turn north, away from the dual carriageway. 'Hang on a sec, that can't be right.' But he had no option but to do as the satnav instructed.

The road wound its way along the side of the valley, through dusty fields and past deserted farmhouses, parallel to the dual carriageway. There didn't seem to be any other cars on the road we were travelling on. Looking at the satnav I could see that this road wound like a snake through fields for what looked like miles and miles before finally joining the main road into Palermo.

'We could turn round if you want?' I was starting to get a bit nervous. That ferry wouldn't wait for us. We had Leonardo's *Last Supper* to see in Milan in two days' time, and I was not going to miss that booking – even if I had to walk back up Italy to get to it.

'We've made it this far,' Frank said. 'I'm not going back now.'

'Is everything okay?' Edith piped up from the back seat.

'Everything's fine, darling.' But I was starting to get a very bad feeling.

We rounded yet another bend and then we saw it: a large sign blocking the road. Our knowledge of Sicilian road signs was not exactly comprehensive. Frank braked.

'What do you think that sign means?' My bad feeling had just worsened.

'Well, to me it looks a lot like "road closed for repairs",' Frank said.

One of the problems with relying on a satnav to do the navigation for you is that you don't know what to do if something goes wrong. I had absolutely no idea where we were on the map. I had long since lost track of which tiny country road we were driving along. Our ferry was due to leave in a few hours. We didn't have time to go back, and we couldn't go on. Or could we?

Frank clearly had the same idea as me. 'Shall we do it? It might not mean what it looks like it means.' He seemed to be saying this more in hope than in expectation.

'No choice,' I said.

'Take a punt?' Frank smiled at me. He likes taking punts.

'Yep.'

'What are you two talking about?' Alfie wanted to know.

'Err, nothing, don't worry,' I smiled at him. Frank got out of the car, shifted the sign to one side a bit, and got back in alongside me.

'Why did you just move that sign?' There was a note of suspicion in Edith's voice.

'No reason, darling,' Frank said, cheerfully.

We carried on driving along the tiny country lane. The road was little more than a farm track now, but at least there didn't seem to be any road works or closures. Perhaps we had misinterpreted the sign. There were no cars, no tractors, no houses, no signs of occupation. Occasionally we would pass a dilapidated stone building, long since deserted. On the satnav screen, all I could see was the winding road snaking its way through the farmland. Nothing else. The contours of the land meant that the rest of the world was hidden from view. It felt like being trapped on an alien planet with no signs of life.

'This is a bit freaky.' Frank crept cautiously onwards. 'I wouldn't like to get stuck in one of these ruts. We could be trapped for days before anyone came past.'

I checked my mobile phone. No signal. A slightly sick feeling had settled in the pit of my stomach. 'This is starting to feel like it might have been a really bad idea.'

'Is everything okay?' Edith piped up again from the back.

'You worry too much,' Frank rounded yet another bend. 'It'll be …' He ground to a sudden halt and yanked up the handbrake.

'What's going on?' The kids wanted to know.

'Nothing.' I gulped. Now we knew for sure what the sign had meant. Ahead of us the rutted farm track had disappeared. It looked like there had been a landslide at some point which had washed away the muddy track completely. There was a massive hole where the road used to be. It was about ten metres long.

'What do we do now?' I checked my watch. Time was fast running out.

To the left of where the road used to be a rough track led around the gaping pit in the road and into the edge of a field until it came out on the other side.

'Look,' Frank pointed. 'It seems like the locals have taken matters into their own hands and created a way round.'

'Frank. Don't you dare!' Frank released the handbrake and began to roll forwards.

'This is where a four-wheel drive car comes in handy.'

'Seriously, Frank. Don't do it.'

Frank ignored me. He inched forwards slowly, gradually turning the car to the left, and climbed up the muddy bank. We were now balanced precariously alongside the enormous hole. The tyres spun slightly in the damp mud. I closed my eyes. If I had been religious, this would have been the point at which I would have started to pray. The car listed to the right and my stomach leapt. The car rocked from side to side for several seconds. Then with a roar of the engine and a squeal of the wheels, Frank made it over the gap and lurched out on the other side.

Ten minutes later we finally reached the dual carriageway. I heaved a huge sigh of relief as Frank put his foot down on the accelerator and we sped off towards Palermo. We had a ferry to catch. And we couldn't be late because we had an appointment to keep with one of the most famous paintings in the world.

This Is the Day

As we walked into the Convent of Santa Maria delle Grazie in Milan, there were a couple of American tourists having a quarrel at the reception desk. They wanted to know why they couldn't just pay and go in to see Leonardo da Vinci's masterpiece.

'But we came all the way from Texas to see it!' the woman complained.

'You must book appointment,' the woman on the reception desk pointed out in a heavy Italian accent.

'But we didn't know that we had to book an appointment!' the man said. 'How were we supposed to know that?'

'Surely we can just pay a bit extra and go in anyway? C'mon, honey, give the lady some cash.' The woman nudged the man, who began to rifle through his wallet. He pulled out a fat wad of euros.

'It's no possible,' the woman said. 'You cannot buy appointment. You must book appointment.' While the Texans continued to argue their case, I stepped up to the other woman on the reception desk and gave her my booking reference. She typed my reference into a computer, printed off some tickets and handed them to me.

'You go and wait in there.' The receptionist pointed to a room off to one side where a group of tourists were waiting to be let into the refectory.

'Hey! That's not fair!' the Texan man shouted. 'They just got here too!'

I was tempted to point out to the man that we hadn't 'just got here'. I was tempted to tell him that we had driven over 5,000 miles. I was tempted to point out that we had traversed Europe, crossed high mountain ranges, travelled the length of the rutted motorways of Italy, nearly been killed in a tragic satnav road closure incident on our way to Palermo, before taking a ferry back up the length of Italy again. And that we had timed our entire adventure around the next fifteen minutes, my daughter's love of Leonardo da Vinci and her desperate desire to see *The Last Supper*. But I didn't. I just smiled at him and we headed off to wait our turn.

'Please step inside the foyer,' a disembodied voice came over a loudspeaker. We shuffled into a small glass walled room along with eleven other people who had booked the same slot as us. The glass door hissed shut behind us. It was like I imagined going into an airlock to get onto a space station would feel. The glass door in front of us hissed open and we stepped into the refectory. There was a collective intake of breath. It was a simple stone built room, frozen in time since the 1500s. The convent was bombed during the war, in 1943, but they sandbagged *The Last Supper* and somehow it made it through. The refectory was completely empty, apart from Leonardo's masterpiece and a set of barriers to stop anyone getting too close. Signs everywhere warned us that we were not allowed to take photographs.

The Last Supper is not especially fancy or decorative. It is a scene of a long, straight dining table scattered with food. Jesus and his disciples are seen in mid feast, with various conversations going on between them, and Judas spilling the proverbial salt (something that only became unlucky after people saw Leonardo's mural). Perhaps it was to do with the latest restoration, or perhaps it was just Leonardo's original genius, but somehow the painting seemed to glow from within. It might have been my fanciful imagination, and all the build-up we had gone through to get to this point, but I'm not sure it was. We stood for a moment breathing in the atmosphere of the simple refectory with its world famous mural. A silence fell over the group. And then the silence was broken by the screeching sound of feedback from a speaker.

I looked across to where the noise had erupted. Our guide was tapping on a microphone. And then she began to speak. It turned out that I had booked a slot with a commentary. On the plus side, the commentary was in English rather than Italian. On the downside, we couldn't understand a word of it anyway, because the acoustics in the ancient refectory meant that our guide's voice echoed up and around the stone room, as though it was pinging off each of the walls in turn. No matter how quietly she whispered, or how loudly she spoke, or how carefully we listened, we could not make out a word of what she was saying. The guide tried valiantly to make herself understood, but it was no use. She might as well have gone 'blah, blah, blah' for all that her commentary added to the experience. In fact, we would have enjoyed the whole thing an awful lot more if she had just stopped talking and let us look at the painting in silence. But I wasn't about to argue after we had made such an effort to get here. I mentally blocked out the noises that were saturating the room, and stared in wide-eyed wonder at the painting. Beside me, Edith's mouth had dropped open. She was staring at her hero's masterpiece in awe.

All too soon our allotted fifteen minutes were up, and we had to exit the refectory. As we left Leonardo's mural behind, I squeezed Edith's hand. I allowed myself a small smile of satisfaction and gave myself a mental pat on the back for being an okay parent. We had made it. We had travelled the length of Italy, and back up it again. Our daughter had made her request, and we had done everything in our power to get her here. We had stood in the presence of Leonardo's genius, even if only for a short space of time. And it had been worth every single second.

Take It Easy

'Can I borrow your new penknife, Alfie?' Edith turned to her brother and deployed her sweetest smile on him. The sun was baking the pebbly beach where we sat on some blankets, taking it easy for the day. We were spending our last bit of time in Italy exploring the beautiful area around Lake Como. The apartment where we were staying not only had two bedrooms (much to Frank's delight) but it was also within walking distance of the lake. Beside the lake there was an excellent sports bar. We were kicking back for a few days.

'What do you want my penknife for?' Alfie looked at his sister suspiciously.

'I want to whittle some sticks.'

'Well, you can't borrow it. I only just got it.'

'No, you didn't. You got it at that shop in Florence outside the Uffizi. And that was before we went to Rome, Naples, Sicily, Genoa and Milan.' She had a point.

'Let your sister borrow your penknife, son,' Frank said. Alfie muttered something under his breath and handed it over grudgingly. His sister set to work, whittling a stick with a sharp point.

I smiled at the tranquil family scene. This was exactly the kind of thing I had been hoping for when we set off on our Road School trip – the sort of educational experiences that require a penknife and a stick, rather than a pen and a bit of paper. I picked up a pebble from the beach and turned it over and over. The pebble felt cool in my hand. It was a perfect round, flat shape.

Now stone skimming was something that every kid should definitely learn, but they don't teach you in school. Unfortunately I was crap at it, but I knew a man who was an expert.

'Frank?' Frank looked at me suspiciously, just like Alfie had looked at his sister ten minutes earlier when she asked to borrow his knife.

'I know that tone of voice. It's the one you use when you want something from me.'

'I've got an idea.'

'I don't like the sound of that.'

'Don't worry. It's about something that you can teach the kids.'

'I've told you. You're the teacher. I'm only here for the lunches.'

I pushed myself to my feet and wandered down to the lake. I took the flat stone and tried to throw it so that it skimmed across the water. It landed with a splash and immediately sunk without trace.

'What are you doing?' Alfie had looked up from the book he was reading.

'Something that I'm crap at, but that your dad knows exactly how to do.'

Frank came over to where I was standing. He bent and picked up a stone. 'Here, let me show you.' Frank threw the stone and it skimmed once, twice, three, four times across the lake, before disappearing with a perfect sploshing sound.

'Show me! Show me!' Both children leapt to their feet and rushed over to where their dad was standing.

'First, you have to pick the perfect stone. This one is just the right shape.' He showed them the one he had chosen. 'Now, you lean slightly back like this, hold your arm horizontally, then as you let the stone go, you flick your wrist very slightly.'

Frank's stone skidded across the surface. This time it jumped five times before it dropped under the water. The kids clapped loudly. I flopped back down onto the picnic rug and watched as Frank taught the kids the correct technique. Although Frank might not be 'a teacher', I thought, when it came to teaching children how to skim stones, he was a natural.

Italian Lessons

1   The history and culture of Italy is deeply interwoven with its landscape. Perhaps the same could be said of all countries, but we felt this particularly strongly when we were in Italy. If you live next to an active volcano, that has got to have an effect on your attitude to life. If you might die tomorrow, 'carpe diem', as the saying goes.

2   Driving is a great way to get around and see the landscape of a country. Sometimes, though, a boat is a more sensible option, and kinder on your tyres, especially given the state of Italian roads.

3   Don't trust a satnav, especially if you've got a ferry to catch or if you're on the side of a volcano. If you do use a satnav, always have a reliable map to hand.

4   Memory is about moments of emotion as well as about sets of facts. We experience the world through what we feel as much as through what we know.

5   One of the best things you can do as a parent to help your children learn is to find out what your child's obsessions are and feed them until they just can't take any more.

6   Learning works best when it happens in real life, because it is multi-sensory and (to state the bleeding obvious) it is *real*. There is no comparison between learning about volcanoes in a classroom, and climbing to the top of a volcano where there is igneous rock under your feet and the smell of sulphur in the air.

7   Following a child's interests is not about limiting their experiences to what they already like, but about giving them access to lots of different experiences until they figure out which ones they love best. For Alfie, Road School was about rocks, fossils, volcanoes and weapons. For Edith, Road School was about art, the natural world, the maths of money and the genius of Leonardo da Vinci. If you introduce children to enough different experiences, they can figure out for themselves what they want to get obsessed with.

8   The idea of spending six months travelling with your own kids, twenty-four hours a day, seven days a week, sounds great. Until you actually do it, that is, at which point you start to appreciate the benefits of being able to send them to school every day.

9   If you go travelling with your kids, try to book at least some accommodation with two bedrooms.

10 Every kid should learn how to whittle a stick and skim a stone, but you don't have to be 'a teacher' to show them how to do it.

An Education

What is 'an education'? Is it about going to school every day, wearing the correct uniform, working hard in your lessons and completing your homework? Is it about doing what your teachers tell you to, being well behaved and compliant? Is an education about how many facts you know and can recall in exams? Or could it be something different — something that can happen out in the world, as well as in a classroom? Road School was an experiment in teaching and learning; it was also about a philosophy of life. This was a chance to break free from the day-to-day routine and go on an adventure with our children. Rather than following a curriculum, we got to follow our interests and explore some amazing places. And we were learning, all the time, even if it wasn't in the same way that we might learn at school.

From the moment you have children, the push is on to get you back into employment, by educating your child elsewhere than at home. In England, parents are offered 'free childcare' for their children, from the term after they turn 3 years old (well before statutory school starting age). Many parents return to work because they want to or because they have to, but some parents decide to stay at home and do the educating themselves. Children are only small for such a short period of time. Before you know it, the years will have flown past and they will be independent adults. Although you might lose out financially if you choose to home educate or go travelling with your children, you will reap dividends in interesting experiences and family relationships. Work and money are not all that matters — if they were, you probably wouldn't have had children in the first place.

In school, your child will be in a class with perhaps twenty-nine other children, and it would be impossible for the teacher to personalise the learning for each one. But when you educate your children yourself, you have the opportunity to follow their lead. Home education is not about a government-designed curriculum taught in specified lesson times. It is not about turning up and doing what you are told. It is about you and your children hunting for learning together. While we were on the road we didn't *have* to do anything, so everything we did was what we *chose* to do. It is tempting to imagine that, given the choice, the children's interests would mostly involve playing on electronic devices while eating junk food. However, this underestimates the intellectual curiosity of children. If you offer them a series of fascinating places and exciting experiences, they would be hard put not to learn.

Parents instinctively follow their children's interests when they are young. If your small child shows an interest in dinosaurs, tractors, horses, frogs or wizards, you go all out to give them experiences related to that topic. You buy them books, read them stories and take them to museums. You count the tractors or horses as they go down the road. You find lots of playful opportunities for learning about the child's favourite things. In the first phase of education (the Early Years Foundation Stage in England) everything is centred on the child. But as children grow older and begin their statutory education, the process becomes more formalised. They are given an agreed diet of literacy, numeracy and other subjects. School starts to have more control over the 'what' and the 'how' of learning, and the child starts to have less.

It is pretty much unheard of for a 3-year-old to be 'disaffected' with education, but it is perfectly normal to talk about a 13-year-old feeling that way. The older children get, the less it seems that school learning is intrinsically motivating in its own right. This is not to say that schools do a bad job – it is not the fault of the people working inside the system. But for a lot of children motivation tends to drop off as they age. Of course, this is partly to do with hormones and peer pressure. As children move into their teenage years, they are influenced more by what their friends think than by what their teachers or parents say. But to an extent the drop-off in motivation is also about an approach to education that says, 'This is what you must learn, and this is how you must learn it.' If we prioritise test results over engagement and curiosity, some children will decide they can't be bothered.

To maintain an intrinsic motivation to learn, we need to:

- Give children an element of choice so that they have a measure of control over their own learning.
- Allow them to make some decisions about what they learn and how they learn it.
- Value learning and intelligence in the widest sense, celebrating what the child can do, rather than focusing on what they can't.
- Let the environment around us be the teacher – there is knowledge in the landscape, the wildlife, the buildings, the culture and so on.
- Give children access to varied experiences and a wide ranging set of

cultural references – take them out into the world in search of learning.

- Figure out, and capitalise on, their interests. When children express a fascination with a particular topic, shower them with resources related to it.
- Help them to follow their interests through to the highest level of detail, exploring a favourite subject in as much depth as time allows.
- Remember that our role can be about easing the children's path towards learning, as well as being an expert who passes on knowledge.
- Immerse children in multi-sensory experiences using approaches to learning that are (at least some of the time) about more than just pen and paper.
- Capitalise on the role that objects and artefacts play in developing a sense of fascination and curiosity and in gaining an insight into different cultures.
- Set targets and offer structures to create a feeling of focus and success – the diaries gave our children a goal to aim for and a format within which to work.
- Make the learning as real as possible – the closer to real life an experience is, the more it will lead to a wide understanding.
- Learn in the outdoors! Not only is this great for children's physical well-being, but fresh air seems to be a great spur for cognitive development as well.
- Consider learning in its widest sense – not just academic development, but experiences that help children learn how to be kind, brave and curious.
- Link the curriculum to the social and emotional aspects of life – for instance, building empathy.
- Find out what makes them happy, and do more of it.

One of the great things about Road School was the way that we could involve the children closely in their own learning. When planning a road trip, encourage your children to tell you where they would like to go, what they would like to learn, and which topics or subjects they are most interested in learning about. Let them read the travel guides, study the maps and do at least some of the decision making. After all, it is their adventure as much as it is yours.

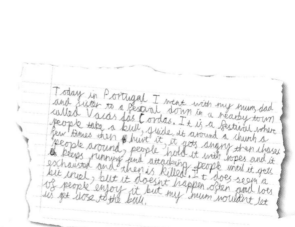

Today in Portugal I went with my mum, dad and sister to a festival down in a nearby town called Vacas das Cordas. It is a festival where people take a bull, guide it around a church a few times then hurt it, it gets angry then chases people around, people hold it with ropes and it keeps running and attacking people until it gets exhausted and then is killed. It does seem a bit cruel, but it doesn't happen often and lots of people enjoy it but my mum wouldn't let us get close to the bull.

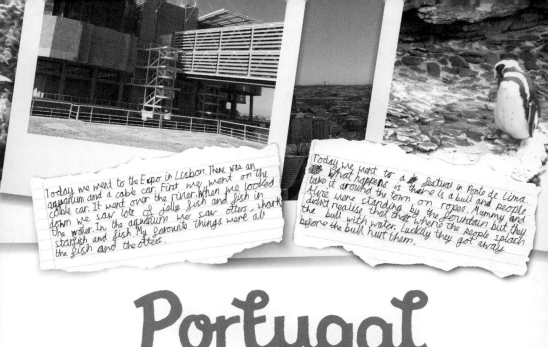

Today we went to the Expo in Lisbon. There was an aquarium and a cable car. First we went on the cable car. It went over the river. When we looked down we saw lots of jelly fish and fish in the water. In the aquarium we saw otters, sharks, starfish and fish. My favourite things were all the fish and the otters.

Today we went to a festival in Ponte de Lima. What happens is there is a bull and people take it around the town on ropes. Mummy and Alfie were standing by the fountain but they didn't realise that that's where the people splash the bull with water. Luckily they got away before the bull hurt them.

Portugal

Cristo Rei

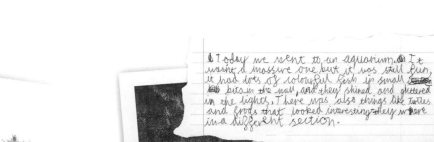

Today we went to an aquarium. It wasn't a massive one but it was still fun, it had lots of colourful fish in small bits in the wall, and they shined and glittered in the lights. There was also things like turtles and frogs that looked interesting they where in a different section.

Bridge Over Troubled Water

It was 1998. Frank and I were both living in Lisbon. In those days, Frank worked for Virgin Megastores, and he had relocated from his job in London to help open a new Megastore in central Lisbon. I had joined him in Portugal, and I was teaching at an International School near Cascais. This was in the days before we had kids, a time when we were free to travel the world without a second thought if a work opportunity presented itself. We had packed up our clothes, our books, our CDs and our cat, and moved lock, stock and barrel to a new country.

'Wow,' I said, turning to Frank, 'that's a pretty amazing bridge.' The new bridge snaked across the river, disappearing into the distance. Its pillars and cables seemed to rise up out of the water like the sails of a boat.

'It certainly is,' Frank said.

We were in the north-east of the city, visiting Expo 98 – the World's Fair. The theme of the Expo was 'The Oceans, a Heritage for the Future', chosen in part to celebrate 500 years since Vasco da Gama discovered the sea route from Europe to India. Earlier that year the new Vasco da Gama Bridge had opened over the River Tagus. The river is very wide at the point where it crosses and it was the longest bridge in Europe, with a span of over ten miles. The bridge was not only a feat of engineering, but it was also stunning to look at.

'Shall we go in now?' I looked down at the tickets I was holding. Frank's job at the Megastore meant that he got showered with free concert tickets. There were lots of great bands playing at the concert venue in the Expo. We had already seen R.E.M. and the Fun Lovin' Criminals, although sadly we'd had to turn down the chance to see Lou Reed. Tonight we were looking forward to listening to Suede.

Fifteen years later, we were driving towards the Parque das Nações, as the area around the Expo is now known, with our two kids in the back of the car. We were staying with the children's Portuguese grandparents, who live just north of Lisbon, for a few weeks of Road School Portuguese style. Since the Expo, the area next to the bridge had been turned into a fantastic leisure park with great restaurants, go-karts, a cable car ride and a massive aquarium. The kids were going to love this.

'The park's just over there.' Frank pointed to our right, where the park spread its way along the bank of the Tagus. The kids peered out of the window.

'That cable car looks cool,' Edith said. 'Can we go on that?'

'Of course you can. Now, if I remember rightly, it was a bit tricky to find the right turning into the park. Not this one,' Frank passed a turning on our right. 'Not this one,' we passed another turning. 'Ah.' There was a long pause. Then, 'Whoops.'

'What do you mean "whoops", daddy?' Edith leaned forward through the gap between the seats. 'Daddy, we seem to be heading for that enormous bridge.' Edith pointed at the bridge, which was now filling the entire front windscreen.

'She's got a point, Frank. Are you sure this is the way?' I looked over to our right where we could see the Parque das Nações below us. We were on an elevated section of motorway, and if I wasn't very much mistaken, we weren't heading for the park. We were heading directly for the Vasco da Gama Bridge.

Frank carried on driving straight towards the bridge. He didn't have any choice at that point because there was nowhere to turn around.

He smiled. 'Hey, it'll be fun.'

'What'll be fun, daddy?' Edith said.

'Your father is taking us ten miles in the wrong direction. Silly Frank,' I tutted.

'Can't we just turn around?' Alfie said.

Frank smiled a smile of sad acceptance. 'Not until we get to the other side.'

Ten miles later, Frank got to the other side of the bridge, paid the toll and drove on to the next motorway junction. Then he exited and turned around.

'You get a great view of Lisbon from this bridge, don't you?' Frank said, pointing to where the city was spread out to our left, as we drove the ten miles back over the bridge. 'That's Cristo Rei over there. It's close to the old bridge over the river. The old bridge is called the 25th of April Bridge, or the Ponte Vinte Cinco de Abril.'

'What's a Cristo Rei?' Edith said.

'It's a huge statue of Jesus, inspired by the one in Rio de Janeiro,' Frank said.

'Why does the bridge have such a weird name?' Alfie said.

'Because it was renamed after the Carnation Revolution in 1974.'

'What's a revolution?' Edith wanted to know.

'And why was it called Carnation?' Alfie added another question to Frank's list.

As we headed back across the river, Frank treated the kids to an impromptu lesson about Portugal. He explained the historic connections between Brazil and Portugal, which led to the building of Cristo Rei. He told them all about the Carnation Revolution, a very Portuguese revolution, in which almost no shots were fired and the people stuck carnations in the muzzles of the soldiers' guns. And he explained how the Salazar Bridge was renamed after the date on which the regime he had begun was toppled. The children were captivated by Frank's stories of Portuguese history. And I was happy to lean back in my seat and close my eyes for a while. At least, I thought, thanking my lucky stars, Frank wasn't playing petrol roulette that day.

The Tide Is High

The aquarium at Parque das Nações is housed in a giant cube shaped building. At the centre of the building is a vast tank containing hundreds of large sea creatures, including some massive and extremely odd looking ocean sunfish. Your journey around the aquarium takes you through four different zones – the rocky coast of the North Atlantic, the cold Antarctic coastline, the temperate Pacific and the tropical Indian coral reefs. The aquarium features pretty much every sea creature you could think of, from both above and below the sea – there are 450 species including penguins, otters, jellyfish, sea horses and starfish.

'Will there be any deadly sea creatures in there?' Alfie asked as we made our way up the long ramp and into the aquarium. Alfie has always had a bit of a thing for dangerous creatures. I think it might have been all the Steve Backshall shows he watched on TV when he was younger. We were going to have to keep an eye out for dangerous stuff while we were in the aquarium.

Alfie leaned against the side of the huge tank at the centre of the building, peering at the giant ocean sunfish that was swimming around inside. Every minute or so, it would pass the point where we were standing. It was huge, and it was the weirdest fish we had ever seen. Although the tank was massive, I felt pretty sorry for that poor fish, swimming round and round in circles, doomed to look at tourists forever more.

'That looks like a reef shark,' Alfie said, pointing at a shark as it swam past us. 'And that's a stingray. They're pretty deadly. And that's a barracuda – it has really sharp teeth, like a piranha.' We carried on along the route through the different zones, admiring the hundreds of different underwater species.

'Starfish are amazing creatures,' Alfie said to his sister. 'If they lose one of their arms, they can regenerate it.'

The kids were both crouched down beside a long slim glass-sided tank. Stuck to the inside of the glass were lots of starfish. The kids touched their fingers against the glass and examined the suckers. I was on the other side of the room, where two sea otters were lying on their backs in the water preening themselves. They were extremely cute. Edith was going to enjoy this once she had finished communing with the starfish.

'Have they got a blue-ringed octopus or a lionfish here?' Alfie said. 'They're really poisonous.'

'They've probably got both.' Frank said.

'Wow.' Alfie smiled. 'This place is deadly. It's even better than when we saw that seagull kill a pigeon in Venice.'

Burning Down the House

Alfie groaned. 'Not another place where you used to live.'
'Do we have to?' Edith joined in the outbreak of moaning.

'Is it going to take ages to find like last time?' Alfie said. It was a fair question, given Frank's nostalgia trip to Kronberg im Taunus.

'No, it's not,' Frank said. 'It's only fifteen years since we lived here. My memory isn't that bad.'

I raised a sceptical eyebrow. 'This place was a bit more special than your dad's home in Frankfurt, though. Wasn't it Frank?'

'It was the most amazing flat we've ever lived in,' Frank said. 'And I found it, because I moved out here first. Your mum just had to turn up and unpack.'

He pulled up outside a nondescript looking building on a small side road and switched off the engine. The building was cream with brown tiles.

'It doesn't look very special to me,' said Alfie.

'Well, that just goes to prove that appearances can be deceptive,' Frank said.

We were in the district of Lisbon known as Graça. Lisbon is a very hilly city – just like Rome it is built on seven hills – and our old flat was at one of the highest points. From the front it looked like nothing out of the ordinary: a block of flats five storeys high, with little to distinguish it from any other block of flats in the nearby streets. But once you stepped inside, you were transported into another world – a light-filled space with the most incredible view of Lisbon you could ever imagine.

The apartment block was built into the side of the hill, so that although from the front it seemed to have only five storeys, half the block was hidden below ground. Under the street level there was a set of storage rooms, an underground car park and a caretaker's flat. When we lived there it had only recently been built and the interior was as amazing as the view – a huge open living area filled with sparkling marble, granite and glass. There was also a large balcony where I grew plants in pots. Our cat used to scramble up a spindly tree that grew out of the built-in window boxes, risking life and limb over the fifty foot drop to the caretaker's terrace below.

'The freakiest thing about this place was the parking,' Frank said to the kids. 'See those gates there? When they opened, you drove your car onto a platform. Then you pressed a button and the lift took you down to an underground car park, two storeys below ground.'

'Woah,' Alfie said, 'that sounds cool.'

'Where's this amazing view, though?' Edith said.

'Through there, on the other side.' I pointed to the flat. It was impossible to see the view from this side because the building itself was in the way, so the kids were just going to have to imagine it.

At that moment, a car pulled up at the block to the left of our old flat. This building had a parking area that wrapped around the back at ground level. The gates to the parking area swung open.

'Follow me, kids,' I said. Frank and the kids scurried through behind me, close on my heels.

'Wow!' both kids stopped in their tracks as they saw what we meant by 'an amazing view'. The whole of Lisbon was laid out before us. You could see the River Tagus weaving its way through the city. You could see the 25th of April Bridge and the statue of Cristo Rei, with his arms out, embracing the city. Far below the distinctive yellow trams of Lisbon were making their way up and down the city streets, dinging as they went.

'I used to get one of those trams into work,' Frank said, pointing.

'And that was our flat,' I said, turning around to look at the back of our building.

'Ah,' Frank said. 'It looks like they're doing some renovations.'

Fifteen years on, the shiny new block of flats where we used to live was a mess. Paint peeled from the exterior walls. The bricks were crumbling. The window boxes had been emptied of their plants. A rusted air conditioning unit hung half off the wall, dripping water. Some Portuguese guys were hard at work inside, ripping out the interior.

Frank turned to me. It might have been my imagination but I could have sworn there was a tear in his eye.

'I still miss that flat,' he said, turning to go. 'It's a shame to see it so rundown.'

'Me too,' I said. 'But it will live on in our memories as one of the best times in our lives.' I put my arm around Frank, gave him a squeeze, and we headed back to the car.

That's Not My Name

Portuguese is an unusual language. It's fairly easy to learn to read it, especially if you know a bit of French or Italian. But learning to speak and hear it? Well, that's an entirely different matter altogether. There are a lot of sounds in Portuguese that have no equivalent in English – not least the 'ão' combination, which appears in many Portuguese words and basically sounds like a cat being strangled. And the place names? Well, just try saying Alfeizerão, Arcos de Valdevez or Coimbra correctly if you haven't got a Portuguese person handy.

We drove into the tiny Portuguese town of Lourinhã, about thirty miles north of Lisbon. In Lourinhã you can find some of the most remarkable fossils in the world, dating from the Late Jurassic period. The fossils were found in the Lourinhã Formation, which is a geological formation on the beach near to the town where dinosaur fossils literally fall out of the cliffs and onto the sand. The town has become famous for its numerous and unusual fossils, and luckily for us (and especially luckily for the dinosaur obsessed Alfie) it was only twenty minutes' drive from his grandparents' house.

'Wow,' Alfie said, as we drove across the roundabout on the outskirts of town. There were three massive metal dinosaur sculptures in the centre.

'Check out the name of that *pastelaria*.' I pointed to a shop we were driving past. It was called Dinopão.

We parked up and piled out of the car. Then we headed into town to find the Museum of Lourinhã. We've had a bit of experience of provincial museums in Portugal, so we weren't expecting the Natural History Museum. In the end, though, we found something even better. The small museum was located in an old stone built house in the centre of town, and it contained lots of unusual fossils. There was a huge cast of a *Triceratops* head. There was large theropod nest containing eggs with embryos inside. And there was a Portuguese guy chipping at a rock with a hammer and chisel in the courtyard outside. Thankfully he was taking the Portuguese approach to health and safety, so we could just stroll up to him and have a chat. He explained about the process for getting a fossil out of a rock, and then he gave the kids an impromptu palaeontology/MFL lesson.

If you think the name Lourinhã is hard to pronounce, then just wait until you hear about the names of the dinosaurs that came from there. There are not one, but two, dinosaurs named after the town. The two dinosaurs were very different – one was a massive carnivore called *Lourinhanosaurus*; the other was *Lourinhasaurus*, a herbivorous sauropod. But their names are so similar, and so tricky to say, that even the Wikipedia entry for *Lourinhasaurus* says 'Not to be confused with *Lourinhanosaurus*'.

'*Lourinhanosaurus*?' Alfie said.

'No. *Lourinhasaurus*,' the man said.

'*Lourinhanosaurus*?' Alfie said again.

'No. *Lourinhasaurus*,' the man said.

Alfie screwed up his face and tried again. '*Lourinhasaurus*.'

'That's right.' The man smiled and gave Alfie a thumbs up. Alfie smiled back. And then we headed back into town. It was time to buy a *galão* and some *pasteis de nata* at the Dinopão shop.

I Won't Back Down

L egend has it that the church in Ponte de Lima, in the Alto Minho region of Portugal, was originally a pagan temple, where the people worshipped a goddess in the form of a cow. The festival of Vaca das Cordas is a remnant of that ancient myth which has filtered down through the centuries into its modern day incarnation. If you ask Google Translate to explain Vaca das Cordas to you, it translates the name as 'cow on strings'. 'Bull on a rope' is probably a closer approximation, although nothing quite prepares you for the reality. The festival takes place on the ninth Friday after Easter, on the day before Corpus Christi. According to my guidebook, during the festival four men dressed as millers drag a bull around the town of Ponte de Lima on four ropes. We were here in the north of Portugal to watch them do just that.

'Let's go and get a viewing spot over there by the fountain,' I said. The kids trailed behind me through the packed town square. 'We should be able to see really well from here.'

'I'm going to stand over there.' Frank pointed to a spot on the opposite side of the square. It was okay for him. When you're six foot five you get a great view however thick the crowd. I just felt sorry for whoever was standing behind him.

Although it was still an hour until the festival began, the town was already rammed with people. Surprisingly, though, there was still plenty of space for us to stand and watch from the steps leading up to the fountain in the centre of the town square. As I took up position with the children in front of me, an elderly woman came over to us. She muttered something in Portuguese, flapped her hands at the children and me, and then wandered off with a troubled look on her face. Although I could speak a bit of Portuguese, whatever she said was beyond me.

'What do you think she was saying, mummy?' Edith said.

'I'm not sure. Maybe something like, "Well done, you've chosen a great spot"?' Admittedly, it was a bit strange that there were so few people standing by the fountain, especially since it seemed like the perfect position to view the festival. I shrugged.

A roar went up as the bull arrived in the town square. Four men held the bull on four ropes, dragging the reluctant animal down the street and through the spectators. As the bull passed them, people would run towards it to goad it, then immediately run away again when the bull strained against its ropes, trying to rush at them. From our slightly elevated position it looked like a Mexican wave of people moving towards the bull and then dashing away again.

'I hope they don't drop the ropes,' Alfie said.

'It'll be fine,' I said.

'Err, mummy. They seem to be coming in our direction,' Edith pointed to the men.

'Don't be silly,' I said. Then I looked again. She was right. The men were definitely dragging the bull towards the fountain. All around us, people were backing off to make way for the raging animal.

I quickly grabbed the kids and dragged them through the crowd and over to the other side of the square where Frank was standing. He had a smirk on his face.

'What's so funny?' I said.

'You should have read the guidebook a bit more thoroughly.' He read us the last part of the listing: 'After dragging the bull around the church and through the town, the millers take it up to the fountain in the town square to splash it with water.'

'Ah, so that's what the woman was saying,' I said. 'I think it's about time I learned to speak Portuguese properly.'

Portuguese Lessons

1   There's no one quite like grandma (and grandpa). If you have family in another country, travel becomes an important part of your life.
2   If you want to understand a country, its people and its culture, you need to learn the language.
3   Living in a country is the best way to learn a language because there are people who can speak it properly all around you.
4   It takes a long time to learn a language, but every language learned has to start with the first few words.
5   If a local flaps her hands at you in a signal that seems to mean 'move', then move, even if you don't understand what she is saying.
6   The traditions of the past create a kind of bedrock on which a society is built. But time doesn't stand still and each generation has to create the traditions anew.
7   Old traditions can evolve perfectly happily into new ones, just like the Expo 98 site evolved into the Parque das Nações, and worshipping a cow goddess turned into Vaca das Cordas.
8   Try pronouncing Parque das Nações or Vaca das Cordas correctly and you'll see what I mean about Portuguese being difficult to speak.
9   Being there, wherever 'there' is, will always beat reading about it.
10 Seize the day and lay those experiences down in your memory, because all too soon you will be stardust.

Travelling with Children

Although it can be stressful travelling with children, the more you travel with them, the more they learn to take it in their stride. There are a lot of positives about travelling with kids. They are very portable, especially once they get past the buggy stage. (I definitely wouldn't have wanted to push a buggy around the bumpy streets of Pompeii or through the crowds of Vaca das Cordas.) Flights are also generally cheaper for small children, and they don't take up as much space as adults in a vehicle either. Although babies are even more portable than children, people tend to have few autobiographical memories below the age of about 2 to 4 years (this is known as 'infantile amnesia'). Although you might have a lovely time travelling with your baby, sadly they won't remember it in later life.

Children are generally very adaptable when you present them with challenges, and travel is a great way to help them learn to cope with change and to become more resilient. When they are constantly on the move, children learn to adjust quickly to a new environment. During our trip, we would arrive at our accommodation, unload our suitcases and settle in. The kids would bounce on their new beds, open their new cupboards and unpack their personal items. Then they would locate the TV remote control, find the Wi-Fi code and accept that this was 'home' for the next few days of their lives. However, do bear in mind that too much change all at once can be exhausting, both for your children and for you, and that being a tourist is hard physical work.

To keep your travels as stress free as possible:

- Give your children the sense that this is their adventure, as well as yours. Encourage them to contribute in practical ways to the planning, the organisation and the daily tasks.
- Aim to incorporate elements of a familiar routine into your day, like you do at home, to create a sense of security for your children – for instance, reading a bedtime story together.
- Get the children to take some familiar items that will help the places you stay in feel safer and more homely. These might include a favourite cuddly or a blanket. *Do not lose the cuddly!*
- Snacks are handy for avoiding boredom on long car journeys. Have a box or bag that can go on the back seat between your children,

and allocate an equal amount of snacks for each child to avoid arguments.

- ⛵ To break up the monotony of long journeys, relive some of the travel games that you used to play as a child. Spotting a particular colour or make of car or playing 'I spy' will make the time pass more quickly.
- ⛵ If your travels take you into Europe, bear in mind that timings on the Continent often work quite differently to the UK. Shops may close for lunch and restaurants may not open until later than you would expect in the evening. You might need to adjust your normal day so that meals happen at the 'correct' time of day for the country you are in.
- ⛵ Take into account the times of day when your children will be tired and what you will do at those times. For smaller children, it can be helpful to match up nap times with occasions when you will be driving somewhere.
- ⛵ If you are visiting a hot country, take into consideration the amount of time you will spend in the heat. Think about the availability of shade on your visits to tourist sites and figure out what you can do to cool down.
- ⛵ Remember that, if your children were at school, they would get weekends and holidays 'off'. When you plan your trip, factor in rest days to give you all time to recover. Of course, there is no need for your 'weekend' breaks to fall on a Saturday and Sunday.
- ⛵ It gets very tiring to be on the move constantly. We set aside times when we stayed in one location for a longer period. If you book an apartment for a week or two, it is cheaper than booking a hotel for a couple of nights, and you will usually have access to more extensive facilities as well.

It is hard going, spending twenty-four hours a day, seven days a week with your own children. Even the most devoted parents need a break from time to time, and equally your children will need a break from you. You might intersperse periods of travel with rest times taken back at your home base, so that your children can catch up with their friends and so can you. We took a break of a few weeks after our trip around Europe before we headed off to China. When you are travelling, you could allocate some days when one parent goes out with the children, while the other parent takes a break. Don't expect things to be all sweetness and light – accept that there will be arguments and days when everyone gets on everyone else's nerves – and that this is perfectly normal.

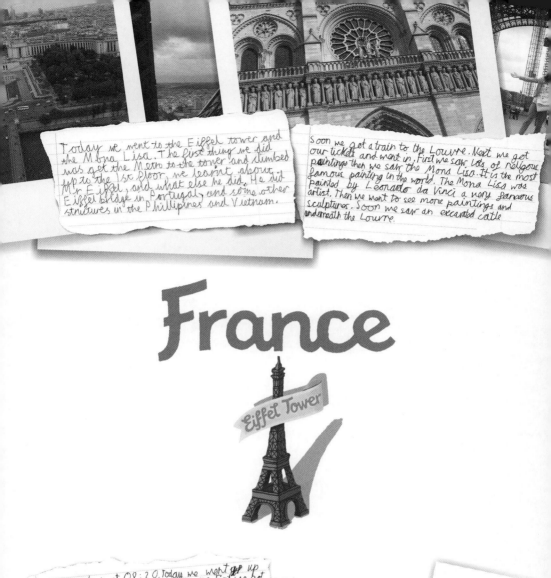

Today we went to the Eiffel tower and the Mona Lisa. The first thing we did was get the Metro to the tower and climbed up to the 1st floor. We learnt about Mr Eiffel, and what else he did. He did Eiffel bridge in Portugal and some other structures in the Phillipines and Vietnam.

Soon we got a train to the Louvre. Next we got our tickets and went in. First we saw lots of religous paintings then we saw the Mona Lisa. It is the most famous painting in the world. The Mona Lisa was painted by Leonardo da Vinci a very famous artist. Then we went to see more paintings and sculptures. Soon we saw an excavated catle underneath the Louvre.

France

Eiffel Tower

Today I got up at 08:30. Today we went up the Eiffel tower and went to the Louvre. First we got a train from Gallieni to Chany de Mars Tour Eiffel. The Eiffel tower is 324 meters high. First we went up 620 stairs. Next we got on a lift from the second floor to the Somment of Paris. Later we got the lift down the Eiffel tower.

Next we went to an art gallery called The Louvre. The first thing we did was go to see the Mona Lisa. Everyone was pushing to see it. It was quite a small picture but it is one of the most famous pictures in the world. My sister wants to learn lots about the artist Leonardo da Vinci.

Stairway to Heaven

Our tour of Europe was finally drawing to a close. We weren't going to be in France for long because we had an appointment to keep with China. So we had made a quick dash up the country and we were pausing for one final stop in Paris. According to Frank, this part of the trip was nothing more or less than a form of torture. He had been here before and he didn't want to be here again. There was nothing I could do or say to persuade him that he needed to see Paris again. Luckily for Frank (or unluckily for him, depending on how you looked at it), he wasn't feeling well. He had holed up in the hotel room for the day with a box of tissues. When the kids asked Frank why he wasn't coming sightseeing with us, he claimed man flu as his excuse. But Frank or no Frank, the kids were going to see Paris, so I had jumped on the Metro with them that morning and headed into the city. We were planning to fit in three of the all-time top Parisian tourist destinations: the Louvre, Notre Dame Cathedral and (of course) the Eiffel Tower.

We stood at the base of the Eiffel Tower and stared up at the top. It looked like a very long way up. The huge metal legs of the tower arched outwards and over us. The area at the base of the tower was crowded with tourists, most of them queuing for the lifts. It seemed an awful lot taller and bigger in real life than it did in the pictures.

'How many steps did you say it was again, mummy?' Edith said, looking towards the top of the tower.

'There are 704 stairs. Almost twice as many as Giotto's Campanile.'

'I really think we should get the lift,' Alfie said.

'C'mon. Don't be such a spoilsport,' I said. 'Think of it as the ultimate PE lesson. Or as our last adventure in Europe.'

'Well, I guess at least this time round I won't have to push dad up when he gets wedged alongside a fat American,' Alfie said, staring up the stairs to where the top of the tower seemed to disappear into the clouds.

We headed towards the entrance to the staircase. There was no way we were going to take the lift. This wasn't because I was feeling energetic but because (a) it was free to walk up and (b) I hadn't got round to booking tickets for the lifts ahead of time, and there was a massive queue.

'It's such a shame daddy felt so ill.' Edith looked sad at the thought.

Alfie nodded. 'He's very unlucky to be missing this.'

'Yeah. You could see how upset he was.' I grimaced.

We took the stairs in batches, pausing for plenty of rests on the way. On the journey up there were lots of signs that told us the story of how the Eiffel Tower was built. The higher we got, the more it started to feel a bit freaky that the metal struts were so easy to see through. As we climbed, Paris got smaller and smaller below us, until the people below looked the size of ants.

Eventually we reached the second section of the tower. We were 115 metres above ground level now, and I was starting to feel the first twinges of vertigo. We waited in line for the lift that would take us up the final section to the top of the tower. We stepped into the glass lift with lots of other tourists and whizzed to the top.

On the final level of the tower you can go outside onto a wind-swept platform to marvel at the view of the whole of Paris. Just below you is the River Seine. Across to your right is Sacré-Cœur Basilica, obvious because of its raised position on the butte Montmartre. Ahead of you is the Arc de Triomphe, with twelve ave-nues radiating out from it. I pointed out the landmarks to the kids as we leaned against the metal barrier that encircled the platform. The railings were dotted with padlocks, many featuring names and love hearts, left by visitors to the tower. I took a few selfies of the kids and me to mark our visit.

'And over there somewhere is daddy,' I said, pointing off to the east of the city where our hotel was located.

'Poor daddy. He doesn't know what he's missing,' Edith said, giving a wave into the distance. 'I wish we'd brought a padlock with us. Then I could have locked it here for daddy.'

'It's such a shame he was too ill to come with us,' Alfie said. 'He must be really upset.'

'Oh yeah,' I said. 'Poor old daddy. He'll be gutted.' I tried to keep the sarcasm out of my voice, but I'm not entirely convinced that I succeeded.

She's Always a Woman to Me

It was easy to tell when we were close to the room that held the *Mona Lisa* because the throng of tourists got thicker and thicker. As we walked into the section of the gallery where da Vinci's masterpiece was housed, we could hardly move for bodies. Ahead of us was a half wall dividing the room in two. On the other side of the wall a massive multinational crowd had gathered, pushing and shoving and holding up cameras and phones. Flashes went off all around the space. The buzz of languages from countries all over the world seemed to fill the gallery with noise. Somewhere, on the other side of that wall, was the most famous painting in the world.

'Woah,' Alfie said.

'Wow,' Edith said.

'It's definitely busy.' I frowned.

'How am I ever going to get to see it?' Edith said. 'I have to see it. This is my last chance to get close to Leonardo.'

'Right kids,' I said, grabbing their hands and pulling them after me, 'let's do this. We're going in.'

We squeezed our way through the heaving mass of bodies and into the Salle des Etats where the painting was kept. A set of barriers had been erected around the space in front of the *Mona Lisa* and there were guards making sure that no one got too close. A bullet-proof screen protected the painting from any attempts at vandalism. Tourists were crushed up against the barriers, snapping photos and chatting loudly about being in a room with the most famous painting in the world. The crowd was bunched so closely together that it was going to be hard for us to position ourselves so that we could actually see it.

The strangest thing about the crowd that blocked our way was that no one seemed to be looking at the picture. They were photographing it, filming it, taking shots of it on their mobile phones and snapping selfies with it, but as far as I could tell, no one was actually admiring the actual painting. It was as though it was more important for them to prove that they had been here, in this room, in the Louvre, with the world famous *Mona Lisa*, than it was to actually look at the painting that had drawn them here in the first place.

Slowly we squeezed our way through, getting closer and closer to the masterpiece. I used the children as a kind of battering ram to drive a pathway through the throng. Eventually we made it to the front, squashed right up against the barriers. And then we just stood there, soaking up this tiny painting that we had driven around an entire continent to visit. We didn't spend the time we were there snapping lots of photos. We didn't take a selfie to prove that we had been in the same room as Leonardo's painting. We just looked at the small picture, and its centuries old model, with her enigmatic smile.

'Apparently the painting was unusual because Leonardo painted her with a smile, and that was something no one had done before,' Edith said. 'Leonardo carried the painting everywhere with him during his lifetime, so he must have really loved it.'

'I bet he never thought that this many people would cram into a room to see it, though,' her brother said.

'I think I will be an artist,' Edith said, as we slipped out of the room and away from the noisy crush. 'Even if I don't earn lots of money or get to be really famous.'

I gave her hand a squeeze and smiled what I hoped was my best enigmatic Mona Lisa smile. 'If that's what you want to do, then of course you will,' I said.

French Lessons

1 When you travel around Europe, France is on the way to a lot of places.

2 Although we can see the appeal of France, our family are not Francophiles. We see it more as a long flat country that you have to drive through on the way to warmer ones.

3 If you spend all your time taking photos of the places you travel to and the things you see, you might forget to enjoy those things when they're actually in front of you.

4 Seeing the best views in life often involves a lot of climbing.

5 It's weird, and rather random, which things get famous and which things don't. Who could have guessed that a tiny painting of a woman smiling would be world famous 500 years later?

6 The idea that something or someone is 'famous' has a funny effect on people. They sometimes stop seeing the thing or the person in its own right, and start seeing the fame instead.

7 If you think the M25 is bad, try driving around the Boulevard Périphérique.

8 The older I get, the more I realise that my dodgy schoolgirl French comes in handy.

9 Paris is only romantic if you haven't got children with you.

10 You can take a man to Paris, but you can't make him be a tourist in it.

Pussycat Parenting

You might have heard of 'tiger mothers' and 'helicopter parents' – parents who push their children to be academically successful, who plan their entire social lives for them and who dictate their every move with the firmest of hands. Our style is probably best described as 'pussycat parenting'. (Although, if truth be told, it is sometimes closer to 'I can't be arsed right now because I'm having a glass of wine' parenting.) This philosophy is not (just) about laziness and a laissez-faire approach to life. We want to encourage our children to become independent thinkers, and that means they need to learn from their mistakes. If they never fail at anything, because we are so busy pushing, controlling and supporting them, they will never learn how to made good decisions on their own. Although part of our role as parents is to protect our children and help them to stay safe, we don't want to be so over controlling that they never get to act of their own volition. We need to put them into situations where they feel challenged and where we don't give them all the answers.

In recent years, there has been a move towards a more authoritarian and controlling approach to schooling – the educational equivalent of tiger parenting. Politicians and educationalists talk about 'high expectations', 'academic rigour' and 'no excuses'. The message is that adults know what is best for children, and that children need to keep quiet and do as they are told in order to succeed. In part, rules are about creating a safe and ordered environment for learning. But there can come a point when the rules lose touch with their original purpose and start to become as much about compliance as about education. While we were on the road, our children went six months without wearing a uniform. This had no negative impact whatsoever on their learning. In fact, the casual clothing they wore might even have helped them to learn, because they felt comfy and relaxed. When you work one to one with your child, on learning that interests them, behaviour is rarely an issue. External controls feel almost irrelevant because the learning is the motivation to behave. In our education system, we have reached the point where some schools specify the exact style of shoes the children wear or how they style their hair. Perhaps we need to ask: what exactly is the educational purpose of this?

When children are used to being controlled by other people, or by external systems, they may struggle in unexpected situations or when there are no adults watching over them. If we can encourage children to think about the *why* of their behaviour, as well as the *what*, they will be better placed to make good decisions for themselves. The challenges that we faced during our road trip helped our children learn how to adapt their behaviour according to different contexts, and how to stay calm when faced with difficulties. Rather than us giving them all the answers, or controlling all the variables, they had to think for themselves.

To support your children in achieving the 'best behaviour' without being over controlling:

- Explore the concept of 'good' behaviour in various contexts – why is it important to behave in this particular way at this specific time?
- Put the emphasis on personal safety, explaining the impact of their behaviour on them and others.
- Talk about how our emotions change relative to the behaviour we encounter – use phrases like, 'It makes me sad when I see you do that' or 'I'm finding that irritating now.'
- Accept that your children's emotional state will affect their behaviour. Help them learn how to stay calm and maintain a sense of perspective.
- Model a measured approach to life's challenges – try not to get wound up, whatever the provocation.
- Be honest about your own shortcomings and be ready to apologise when you get it wrong.
- Accept that you will sometimes be in a bad mood or behave badly. Explain to your children that you are human too.
- Encourage children to assess risk, to be brave and to take some chances.
- Put them in challenging situations where they are taken outside their comfort zone.

The other great thing about not being too pushy and over controlling with your children is that it gives you time to focus on your relationship as well as on your kids. Parenting is a bit like the safety demonstration on an aircraft: adults, fit your own oxygen mask first, before you help your children. Take care of your relationship, and your partner, because that way you will be in the best position to be there for your kids. Work as a team and give each other the space to grow and develop, as well as to act as 'mum' or 'dad'. And if your partner's version of a midlife crisis is to take the kids out of school and go travelling with them, why not go along for the ride?

Another one of my favourite parts of China was the Aqua park in Beijing which is known as one of the best in the world. It had lots of slides but there were 3 really fun ones, one were you ride on a small ring with someone else down a sort of drain. Another one was the Hurricane, it was a massive slide with a large ring you go in with 4 people in total, you go through a small pipe then it drops you into a huge one, which makes you go up both sides. The last was just a larger normal slide but it was still fun. There was also a pool which sometimes made waves, it even announced that it was making waves and had a camera that showed up on a screen.

In China one of the best things we did was going to see the great wall. We hired a private car to take us up there, it was quite nice especially the air conditioning. We where taken up the hill with the wall na ski lift it was quite scary because of how much it blew around and the drop was quite far but it still had a nice view. At the top we walked across the wall, it was quite a long walk but it was still a good one. My favourite part was the ride down, it was a toboyan that was amazing fun. Although there were quite a few rules on it. It started to lightly rain so my mum and sister had to wait but me and my dad went down fast, so fast that my dad crashed into someone, luckily they weren't angry and didn't get hurt too badly I think ...

Today we went to the great wall of China. First we got on a ski lift to the wall. It is very long. It was created to keep Mongolians out of China. Near the end of it we saw Chinese symbols that looked like an x. It was very hot. We saw an old cannon too. On the way down we had to tobogan down but it started to rain so Mummy had to wait.

China

Forbidden City

Today we went to see the Terracotta Warriors. They are an army of terracota soldiers. There were horses, soldiers and other army things. They were all buried in the ground. They were made for an emperor. While we were there I bought two boxes of mini soldiers. I want to give them to my friends. The army was impressive.

Paperback Writer

We were back from our trip around Europe, taking a brief rest before we headed east. Our flights to China were booked. Our vaccinations were done. Now all that was left to do was to sort out the visas.

'You put *what* in my visa application?' I exclaimed. Frank had completed our visa applications for China and sent them away to be processed. According to him, he had been doing me a 'favour'.

'I put that you're a writer, of course. That is what you do for a living, isn't it?'

'Well, yes. But you do realise that the Chinese don't exactly like writers, don't you? I train teachers as well. You could have put that instead.'

'Oh don't be so silly,' Frank said. 'They're not going to ban you from coming to visit their country just because you're a writer.'

'I sincerely hope not. Because otherwise we've just wasted a fortune on flights we can't use. Either that, or you and the kids are going to China without me.'

'Our visas have been approved,' Frank waved a piece of paper at me. 'Do you want the good news or the bad news?'

'What do you mean "the bad news"?' I said. 'If the visas have been approved then we're good to go, aren't we?'

'Well, I'm good to go, and so are the kids,' Frank smiled. 'We have an unlimited entry visa to visit China that lasts for three months. That's the good news.'

'That's great,' I said. 'Why can I feel a "but" coming?'

'Well, you know how I put that you're a writer on the visa application form?'

'Yes.' I didn't like the sound of this.

'You were right. They don't like writers.'

'And?'

'You have exactly thirty days to get in, see China and get back out again. Not a day more. And if you're not gone in time, then you're in serious trouble.'

'Well done, Frank,' I said. 'I guess we'd better not miss our flight home.'

Leaving On a Jet Plane

'Woah!' Alfie's eyes had popped open so wide it looked like they might burst.

'Awesome!' Edith plonked herself down in her seat and started to examine the array of technology that was available on the Aeroflot Airbus A330. Although our kids had spent a lot of time in aeroplanes during their lives, they had only ever flown short haul up to now. The plane that was going to take us from London Heathrow to Moscow, and then from Moscow to Beijing, was a whole different kettle of fish.

'Can we choose from all these movies?' Alfie wanted to know, plugging in his headphones and tapping away at the screen in front of his seat.

'That's the general idea,' Frank said.

'It's going to be a very long flight,' I said.

'*They have the Lego movie!*' Alfie shouted to Edith, at top volume.

'*No way!*' she shouted back, just as loudly. She had plugged her headphones in too and she was rapidly swiping the touch screen in front of her.

'*Yes way!*' Alfie screamed with delight.

The people in the row in front of us turned round, craning their necks to see what was going on. I made an embarrassed face and offered a whispered 'sorry'.

When *The Lego Movie* first came out, we were visiting family in Portugal. We took the kids to see it, but they were unimpressed because it was dubbed into Portuguese. Now they had the chance to watch the original version. And with thirteen hours of flying time ahead of us, they could watch it as many times as they liked.

The plane's engines roared, we sped off down the runway and lifted into the sky. We were on our way. Leaving on a jet plane, heading east to a completely new place, somewhere none of us had ever been before.

Thirteen hours later, after a stopover in Moscow, a lot of snacks and the occasional snooze, the plane finally touched down in Beijing. Alfie unplugged his headphones and smiled. He rubbed at his eyes.

'*The Lego Movie* was awesome,' he said.

'Totally awesome,' Edith said.

'How many times did you watch it?'

'Three times. How about you?'

'Ten.' Alfie turned to me. 'Mum, will they have the same movies on the way home? I want to watch *The Lego Movie* again.'

'I think they probably will,' I shook my head and smiled.

We unclipped our seat belts, pulled our hand luggage out of the overhead lockers and joined the queue of people waiting to leave the plane. And as we made our way off the aircraft and through the airport, Edith and Alfie kept singing to themselves, over and over again, 'Everything is awesome. Everything is cool when you're part of a team.'

'Thanks for the ear worm, kids,' I said, as we climbed into a taxi and headed for our hotel.

'Everything is awesome!' Edith sang, turning to me with a smile.

Stranger In a Strange Land

One of the first things that we obviously had to do when we arrived in Beijing was to visit Tiananmen Square. Not long before we left for China it had been the twenty-fifth anniversary of the protests in the square. The iconic image of a man standing in front of the advancing tanks had been everywhere in the media. Now that we were here, even the idea of talking about the protests seemed foolhardy. Especially since I had already been marked down as 'a writer' on my visa.

Security was tight in the train stations. We had to pass our bags through an airport style security scanner as we entered the subway. There were police everywhere you looked. The atmosphere was subdued. It all felt very alien and strange.

We came out of Tiananmen Dong station and passed through a tunnel that took us under the main road and into the square. It was desperately hot and humid. For most of our visit to China, a thick and choking smog would sit like a blanket over the country, coating it in a relentless grey. But on our first few days of exploring this strange new place, the sky was clear and blue and the sun was mercilessly hot.

The square itself was a huge, open space – acres of grey concrete with no colour in sight. In the centre was a tall granite monument, and behind the monument was Mao's mausoleum. There was not a scrap of shade to be found anywhere. It hadn't occurred to me to bring any hats when we headed out that day.

'I'm boiling.' Edith flapped a hand listlessly in front of her face.

'Me too,' Alfie said.

'Me three.' Frank wiped the sweat from his brow. His t-shirt was already soaked through.

A small Chinese woman came over to where we were standing, dragging a tiny boy behind her. The boy was smiling shyly. The woman held a camera in her hand. She pointed at our children, then at her child, and finally at the camera. Then she smiled a wide, toothy grin and spoke quickly in Mandarin, gesturing again as she did so. We didn't understand a word she was saying, but it was obvious from her hand signals that she wanted to take a photo of our children with her son. I looked at Frank.

'What should we do?' I said. 'Should we let her take a photo?'

'It's probably a scam,' Frank said. 'She'll take the photo and then demand money for it.'

I shook my head at the woman and Frank flapped her away. She scurried off. Moments later, another Chinese family came up to us, dragging another small child. This time the father indicated that he wanted to take a photo of his child with ours. Again we shook our heads and the family moved away.

The fifth time this happened we finally gave in. I shoved Alfie and Edith towards the smiling Chinese family and they snapped several shots of their child with our two kids.

Over the course of the next month this would happen again and again. After a while we figured out that, although it was a bit irritating, it was perfectly normal for Chinese people to ask Westerners if they can take a photo of their children with yours. The Westerners who visit their country are a source of fascination for them. We are the ultimate strangers in a strange land. And because of the Chinese one child policy, our two kids were the ultimate novelty.

Another Chinese family hurried over in our direction, dragging a small and reluctant child behind them.

'Smile,' I said to the kids, pushing them both forwards to get their picture taken. 'You're on camera. Again.'

Here Comes the Sun

As we completed our tour of Tiananmen Square, it felt like we were in an oven. There were huge sweat patches under our arms. The children looked like they were about to melt. I hadn't counted on there being no shade, nor on the sun being quite this hot. We were going to cross back under the main road and tour the Forbidden City next. And from what the guidebook said, there wasn't an awful lot of shade available in there either.

'Daddy, daddy, can we have one of those?' Edith pointed to a wizened old man selling hats. These weren't just any hats though. These were umbrella hats. Rainbow umbrella hats. They had an elastic band that fixed around your head and a rainbow coloured umbrella that opened above your head.

'It might be a good idea,' I said to Frank. 'It is very, very hot.'

'Right then, let's do this,' Frank said, heading towards the man.

Before we flew to China, we had read all about how you had to bargain for everything. How it was considered rude not to try to negotiate a better price. And Frank was about to have his very first go at bargaining by buying some rainbow umbrella sun hats on our first full day in China.

Frank pointed at the hats. 'How much?'

'Fifty yuan.' The old man opened up an umbrella sun hat, passed it to Frank and smiled broadly.

'Fifty yuan!' Frank turned to me and raised his eyebrows. He examined the hat, which quite frankly looked like it probably cost about 20p to produce.

'That's much too expensive.' I said. To be honest, given how hot it was, I would have been quite happy to pay five quid each for the hats. But when in China, you must learn to do as the Chinese do. And the Chinese like to bargain. I was no expert at haggling, but I knew that the best strategy was to try to look as disinterested as you could.

Edith grabbed the umbrella hat from her father and put it on.

She smiled a massive smile and gave us a twirl.

'Don't put it on yet,' I hissed. 'Look like you don't want it.'

'But I love it!' Edith really wasn't getting the idea of this. 'I definitely want one! I'm going to call it a sumbrella!'

'I want one as well,' Alfie said. The man opened another hat and handed it to Alfie. He put it on his head and smiled. 'This sumbrella is great. How do I look?'

The old man raised a thumb at Alfie and held out his hand to Frank for payment.

'We're not very good at this bargaining thing yet, are we?' I said.

Frank fished in his pocket, pulled out some money, peeled off two fifty yuan notes and handed them to the man. The old man smiled broadly, his smile as warm as the midday Chinese sun. Then he tucked the notes into his pocket and shuffled away at top speed, before we could change our minds.

Sailing

After a long, hot but fascinating tour of the Forbidden City, we took the exit out of the city on the north side. Jingshan hill rose up in front of us, jutting into the clear blue sky. The artificial hill was created almost a thousand years before, during the Liao and Jin dynasties. It was built using the soil that was excavated to form the moat around the Imperial Palace. The guidebook told me that the hill was the perfect viewpoint from which to look back over the Forbidden City. The hill had five peaks and on top of each peak was an elaborate pavilion.

We trudged up the hill until we reached the best spot to look back down on the Forbidden City. From this angle you really got the sense of how the city was laid out, with the large rectangular temples in the middle section and the smaller court buildings on either side. I snapped a few photos.

'That's where I want to go next!' Edith was pointing off to the west where there was a large park in the distance. The park had a massive lake dotted with lots of tiny boats.

I consulted my guidebook. 'That's Beihai Park. It looks good. It's got a lake that covers more than half of the park, and it's home to the White Pagoda and the Nine-Dragon Wall. We can visit it tomorrow.'

The next day dawned hot and humid. The sky was still a bright blue, but on the horizon a grey pall of smog had started to rise up on the edges of Beijing. Over the next few days the smog would creep across the city until it was entirely blanketed in the stuff, like a scene from *The Fog*. We took the subway into the centre of town and made our way to Beihai Park, sweating as we walked.

As soon as we entered the park, the kids rushed over to the dock where you could hire boats. Frank paid the man and we were shown which boat we should take.

'Jump in,' I said, hopping into the small battery powered vessel. The kids stepped in and took a seat. Frank jumped in and the boat rocked from side to side, almost tipping over with his weight.

'Kids, you sit on this side of the boat with me,' I said. 'Frank, you sit over there.' With three of us on one side, and Frank on the other, the boat just about balanced out. As long as no one made any sudden movements, we should be fine.

'This looks simple enough,' I said. All you had to do was press down on the accelerator for the boat to move forwards, then ease off for the boat to stop. 'Do you kids want to drive?'

The kids looked thrilled. 'I want to drive it first!' Alfie said.

'No! Me first!' Edith said.

'I asked first!'

'But I'm the youngest, I should go first!'

'That's not fair!'

'Yes it is!'

Alfie got up and tried to jump into the driver's seat. Unfortunately, at the exact same moment, so did Edith. The kids began to shove each other, each trying to claim the seat. We rocked precariously from side to side, dirty lake water slopping into the boat and pooling at our feet.

'Thanks, kids,' Frank said, looking down at the bottom of his jeans which were soaked in lake water. After five more minutes of squabbling, it was agreed that the kids would take it in turns. Alfie would go first, his age giving him seniority, then after five minutes Edith would take over.

Alfie pushed his foot down on the accelerator as hard as he could. The boat moved forwards at a snail's pace.

'It's not very fast,' he said, turning around to lodge his complaint.

'Good,' Frank said.

'Look where you're going!' Edith said. 'Watch out for that boat!'

It was too late. Our boat crashed into another boat coming in the opposite direction. A group of Chinese people in the boat shouted angrily at us.

'Whoops,' Alfie said.

After five minutes, it was time for the kids to swap over. This was a delicate manoeuvre because, with Frank in the boat, we had to somehow balance out the weight while the kids changed places. As we swapped seats, the boat lurched from side to side yet again. The murky lake water slapped the sides of the boat and slopped over the edges. Then, as Edith dropped into the driver's seat, there was a loud splosh. Frank looked down at his jeans. He had a massive wet patch on his lap.

'Classy,' I said. Frank scowled.

Half an hour later the kids had had enough of the boat, and Frank had had enough of getting soaked every time they swapped places. We docked and hopped out, with Frank nearly ending up in the water again. Then we headed off to explore the park, stopping first to look at the White Pagoda on Jade Flower Island, then heading onwards to admire the Nine-Dragon Wall.

The Nine-Dragon Wall was built in 1402 and it did exactly what it said on the tin. It had dragons on both sides, nine of them, modelled in relief along the wall. The sculpted green and blue tiles glistened in the sunshine, the dragons seeming to writhe their way down each side.

'Can we do those next?' Edith pointed to a spot halfway down the lake, back towards the entrance, where some circular boats in the shape of lotus flowers were spinning around on the water.

'Back to the boats again?' Frank sighed. 'My jeans have only just dried out.' The kids rushed ahead towards the boats. We trailed behind. Frank paid the man for half an hour's boat hire, then we headed out onto a wooden pontoon to get into our boat.

Once again, we put the kids in charge of driving, but this boat was quite different to the previous one. Put it this way, boats normally have a pointed bit, so you can point them and they go in that direction. But these circular boats had a mind of their own, especially once our kids had got their hands on them.

And so it was that we found ourselves spinning round and round on the lake in Beihai Park in a lotus flower.

'This brings to mind a song, Frank,' I said.

'Which one's that then?'

'I am sailing!' I sang, grinning. I was starting to feel dizzy and a bit light headed.

'I am sailing!' Frank joined in.

Edith put her fingers in her ears. Alfie carried on spinning the lotus flower.

'Home again!' I shouted at the top of my voice.

'Cross the sea!' Frank shouted back at me, even louder. A group of Chinese people in a boat close by gave us odd looks.

Then I joined in with Frank, and we both sang together at full volume, much to our children's disgust.

'I am sailing, stormy waters, to be near you, to be free!'

Cigarettes and Alcohol

'What are we doing for dinner tonight?' The kids were thinking about their stomachs, again. We had tried the Chinese restaurant in the hotel on our first night there. The food had been decent but nothing special. We had found an amazing Beijing roast duck restaurant, just up the road from our hotel, where we had feasted on all kinds of fantastic Chinese foods. We had visited one of the subway franchises that were dotted around the city to satiate our children's desire for 'something normal to eat'. But tonight we fancied something different.

'Let's go downstairs and see what's available,' I said. 'Maybe the guy on reception can recommend another good restaurant close by.'

We made our way down to the foyer. The receptionist was deep in conversation with a Chinese businessman who was checking into the hotel. The door to the Chinese restaurant was to our right. To our left was another door that I hadn't noticed before. The door had a sign on it. I looked more closely at the sign. It seemed to have the words 'Belgian Bar' written on it. I rubbed my eyes and looked again. It felt like the sign might have just appeared by magic.

'Does that sign say what I think it says?'

'Surely not?' Frank said, looking in the direction that I was pointing. 'It's got to be worth a try though.' He trooped off towards the door, the rest of us trailing in his wake.

When Frank and I were younger we used to visit Belgium a lot. We had a Belgian friend, and we made regular trips to the small, unassuming country. One of the things we both enjoyed a great deal about Belgium was the Belgian bars. The Belgians have a vast selection of different beers – over a thousand – many with their own special glasses. Hoegaarden and Cristal and Leffe. Duvel and Jupiler and Lucifer. We had spent many a night in Belgium when we were younger, sampling the different flavours and getting exceedingly drunk. Frank and I stood at the entrance for a moment, unsure about whether we should risk going in and being disappointed. I mean, there couldn't really be a Belgian bar, could there, here in a hotel on the edge of Beijing? We pushed through the door, the kids following behind us, and it felt like we had entered a parallel universe.

The room was dimly lit and a haze of smoke hung in the air. It was smoky because there were loads of people in there, smoking. That was the first surprise. To our right was a long wooden bar. The bar was lined with every different type of Belgian beer you could possibly imagine. They had all the special glasses too, which was the second surprise. The polished crystal sparkled temptingly in the dim lighting. And not only was there a vast array of Belgian beer, but there was also a pool table and, just to top it all off, table football as well. Three surprises in one go.

'Cool!' Alfie's eyes shone with delight. He hurried over to the table football, his sister following at his heels.

'Amazing,' I said.

'What will it be, madam?' Frank did a deep bow.

'I think I might have a Hoegaarden,' I said. 'But then we really should go and get something to eat.' I remembered from experience just how strong the Belgian beer was, and just how easily it slipped down one's throat.

At that moment, a passing waiter handed me a menu. I flicked it open and discovered that not only were we in the most amazing Belgian bar we had ever been to, but they also served all the children's favourite kinds of foods.

'Does anyone fancy hotdog and chips?' I said, calling over to them.

'Definitely!' Alfie and Edith shouted.

'Or you can have a cheese toastie instead, if you like?' I said.

'Who's up for a game of pool?' Frank said, returning to the table with two glasses brimming full of Hoegaarden and two Cokes with ice.

'*Me! Me!*' both the children screamed at top volume. It looked like this was going to be a very late, and a very pleasurable, night.

China In Your Hand

The kids had informed us that, while we were in China, one of the things we definitely had to do was to go and see some pandas. The giant panda is, after all, emblematic of China.

'Pandas are so cute!' Edith had said, over and over again, from the moment we got back from Europe and told the kids about our next destination. It seemed that she had transferred her obsession from Leonardo da Vinci to *Ailuropoda melanoleuca*. You had to hand it to the kid, she liked to get obsessed by things with long names. Unfortunately, we didn't have time to fit in a trip to the Chengdu Panda Base, where tourists could see pandas in a semi-wild environment. Fortunately, though, we could still go to see the pandas in Beijing Zoo.

'I'm not going to the bloody zoo,' Frank scowled at me. 'I hate zoos.'

'I'm not exactly keen on them either. But it's not always about what we want, Frank. Sometimes it's about the kids. And they want to see some pandas. We are in China, after all.' Frank made a har-rumph sound but wisely decided not to argue.

Just as we arrived at the zoo, a torrential rainstorm started, water pouring from the sky as though someone had emptied a bucket over us. Luckily, three stalls had popped up just outside the zoo, all willing to sell us long plastic raincoats for as many yuan as they could possibly charge us. We were wise to the bargaining thing by now though. The raincoats were advertised at twenty yuan, but after a tense five minutes of hard-nosed bargaining, Frank managed to get the man down to five. We slipped on a raincoat each and headed into the zoo. Immediately, the rain stopped, the sun came out and the raincoats started to act like miniature saunas. I could feel the sweat running down my back. I stripped my raincoat off. Frank and the kids followed suit.

'Can you carry these for us, mummy?' The kids dumped their sopping wet macs into my arms, soaking my top and trousers.

'Thanks kids,' I said.

As we wandered around Beijing Zoo, we realised there were two categories of animals here: there were the pandas and then there was everything else. Most of the zoo was ageing and run-down. Depressed looking animals wandered around concrete enclosures that were far too small for them, or sat listless and forlorn in the heat. But the pandas were different. The pandas were special. While the other animals lived in a grotty bed and breakfast, the pandas lived in a five star hotel in Park Lane. We made our way into the panda area through a series of tall concrete arches. Inside the building was a string of glass-fronted enclosures, giving visitors a perfect view of the pampered residents inside.

'Aww,' Edith said. 'That is so cute.' She pointed to the enclosure where a fat panda was slobbed out, chewing leaves off a piece of bamboo.

The kids hurried over to the first glass enclosure and leaned against it, staring in wide-eyed wonder at the huge black and white bear inside.

The panda yawned. It completely ignored them. It lolled on its back, picking up bamboo stems one after another in its paws and stripping them of their leaves. It yawned again and scratched its bottom. Then it continued to chew aimlessly on the bamboo, completely disinterested in the rows of visitors staring through the glass at it.

'If you ask me, that panda looks an awful lot like a person in a panda suit,' Frank said.

'Maybe it is.' Frank was right. It did look like a bloke wearing a furry black and white suit. I leaned in closer to check. The panda burped loudly.

'Oh, they're so cute,' Edith said.

'They're bears,' Alfie said.

'And?'

'Bears are dangerous. Grrr!' Alfie roared at his sister. Edith shrieked and ran over to me.

'They are cute, aren't they mummy? Daddy?'

'Well, some people might think so. But you wouldn't say that if you saw what this one's doing.' Frank was peering through the glass into yet another enclosure, where yet another panda lived in pampered luxury.

'Why, what is it doing?' Edith went over to where Frank was standing. The panda was hunched over in the corner, spasms running through its body. 'Is it okay? It seems to be shaking. Poor thing. Do you think we should tell someone?'

'Err, I think it's being sick,' I said. As we watched, the panda regurgitated the bamboo it had just eaten, leaving a steaming pile of panda puke on the floor in front of it.

'Yuk!' Edith said. She watched the panda, transfixed. 'What's it doing now?' The panda bent down and fished through the pile of sick it had just deposited.

'Err, it appears to be inspecting its own sick,' I said.

'And now it's starting to eat it,' Frank said, as the panda began to tuck into the pile of lukewarm vomit.

'That is disgusting,' said Edith. She wrinkled up her nose. 'Do you know what? I've changed my mind. I don't think pandas are cute any more.'

Hit Me With Your Rhythm Stick

The bullet train sped out of Beijing and turned inland towards the ancient Chinese capital of Xi'an. We were heading to Xi'an to visit one of the 'must sees' of any trip to China: the Terracotta Army. The train was going to take us the 756 miles between the two cities in just over five and a half hours. I looked out of the window as the train left Beijing and gradually picked up speed. Alongside the railway line the buildings were thinning out, and now there were paddy fields, rice growing in the water. An electronic counter on the wall showed our speed in kilometres. The counter went up and up and up, inching its way from 100 kilometres an hour, to 200 and then up to 300. The train ran so smoothly that it felt like we were flying.

'This train has plugs!' Alfie turned to his sister, with a massive grin on his face.

'Excellent!' she said. They plugged in their electronic devices, stuck their headphones on and booted up their tablets.

'Don't you want to enjoy the view?' I said. There was no answer. The kids were tapping away on their screens. A noise erupted from the seat behind me. I turned around to see what was going on. Frank was fast asleep, snoring loudly. A silvery trail of drool trickled out of his mouth and down his chin. An elderly Chinese man was sitting beside him looking disgruntled. He was muttering away under his breath in Mandarin.

Xi'an is a walled city. The wall that visitors see today was built in 1370, during the Ming Dynasty. The taxi drive from the train station brought us through miles and miles of new tower blocks that were in the process of being constructed outside the main city. As soon as we drove through the city gate, into the old city of Xi'an, there was a sense of being cocooned within its walls. The taxi driver drove up and down the streets looking for the address we had given him. Finally, he pulled up outside a smart looking hotel and we all clambered out.

As well as the obvious delights of the Terracotta Army, one of the highlights of any trip to Xi'an is a visit to the Drum Tower, and that was the plan for our first day in Xi'an. The Bell Tower and the Drum Tower are located at the central axis of the city, and they were both built in the 1380s. The bell in the Bell Tower was struck to mark the dawn, while the drum in the Drum Tower was beaten at sunset to signal the end of the day.

A sign told us that we could enjoy a drum show at the Drum Tower, so we had a quick look around the drum museum that took up most of the central area within the tower, and then we took our seats and waited for the performance to begin.

A group of men and women raced onto the stage, clad in long white trousers and silky white tops, and began to beat some drums rapidly. The next fifteen minutes passed by in a whirlwind of drumming, dancing and rhythmic beats. I felt exhausted by the time it had finished. The drummers exited the stage, sweat pouring from their bodies.

'That was great,' Edith said.

'I wish I could have a go on the drums,' Alfie said.

'You could always take up drum lessons when you start secondary school,' Frank said.

'I'm not sure that's such a good idea.' I could just imagine what our neighbours would say if our son started bashing a drum kit at all hours of the day and night. We weren't exactly the most musically gifted of families.

'Alfie! Alfie!' Edith had gone over to the door where you could walk out onto the terraces that lined the sides of the Drum Tower. 'Come and look at this!'

Alfie hurried over to the doorway where she was standing, then both our kids slipped outside. A few seconds later, I heard a loud and not very rhythmic banging noise.

I went outside to see what was going on. Both of the kids were racing along the side of the Drum Tower, banging randomly on the massive drums that lined the terraces. Frank joined me and we laughed at the racket they were making.

'Our kids might not have much in the way of rhythm,' Frank said, 'but they certainly know how to make a noise.'

Bicycle Race

My guidebook told me that one of the very best ways to see Xi'an was for us to get up on the wall via one of the four gates, hire some bikes and cycle around the perimeter. From an elevated position up on the wall you could look down and see the entire city, or at least you could if the smog wasn't doing its pea-souper thing at the time. The perimeter of the wall was just over eight and a half miles long in total, with gates in the middle of each of the four sides and watchtowers on each corner. The thickness of the wall meant that it gave you a lovely flat wide pavement on which to cycle.

As we entered the wall via the south gate, a troop of soldiers was marching around an open courtyard. They were dressed in traditional Ming warrior costumes made out of overlapping black leather plates and they had long swords attached to their belts. Bright red plumes of feathers adorned their helmets. At the head of the procession was a soldier dressed in a gold version of the costume. We watched as the warriors marched up the stairs to the wall, did a circuit and marched back down again on the far side. It looked like very hot work being a Ming warrior, especially with the thick layer of smog that was sitting over the city and trapping the heat in place.

We climbed up the stairs that the Ming warriors had just come down, and went over to the bicycle hire stall. The bikes were all too high for Edith, so we hired one bike each for Frank and Alfie, and a tandem for Edith and me. I was excited about the idea – I had never been on a tandem before but I had always fancied riding one. Our bike hire would last for 100 minutes, which apparently was just enough time to get around the wall if you went at a moderate speed. As I tried to get to grips with balancing the tandem, and Edith tried to get to grips with reaching the pedals, the two boys raced off into the distance on their bikes.

'Wait for us!' I called after Frank and Alfie, but they were already too far away to hear me.

'That's not fair,' Edith said as we tried yet again to balance ourselves on the bike and pedal it simultaneously.

'Ah, yes, but what they forgot is that today I have the snacks and drinks.' I held up the backpack. Edith giggled.

Eventually we figured out how to balance, and we set off at a gentle pace in a clockwise direction around the wall. Looking over to our right, we could see the entire city of Xi'an laid out below us. But the haze was thick and getting thicker. The middle of the city was already disappearing into a grey fog. It felt very calm and peaceful up on the wall, high above the busy streets. There were hardly any tourists around, just a few bikes whizzing past us as we trundled along. Every so often we would take a break for a drink and a snack and to cool ourselves down. It was far too hot to go at a fast pace, but at least the wall was flat.

Twenty minutes later we made it to the first watchtower on the south-west corner of the wall. Frank and Alfie were sat on a bench, looking sweaty and bored. We drifted to a halt, got off our tandem and leaned it up against a wall.

'What kept you?' Frank said.

'Where have you been?' Alfie said. 'I need a drink.' He grabbed the backpack from me and started fishing around inside.

Frank downed half a bottle of water and Alfie drank a full can of Coke. Then they both hopped back on their bikes and sped off at top speed into the distance. Edith and I had a quick wander around the watchtower, then we settled ourselves back on our tandem as precariously as before, and set off at a relaxed pace. A gentle breeze ruffled our hair as we drifted along, enjoying the view over on our right hand side.

The same scene would replay itself another three times during our trip around the wall. The boys would dash ahead and get to the next watchtower ages before us. We would coast along sedately, keeping our cool. When we arrived at where the boys had parked up, they would be sitting there sweating. They would proceed to complain long and loud about how hot and bored they were, and how slow and irritating we were being. Finally they would glug some drinks and race off again at top speed.

As we finished the final leg of our journey, coming in at 99 minutes (well behind the sweaty boys), I began to serenade Edith. I sang her the song that had been stuck in my head ever since we first picked up our tandem: 'Daisy Bell'. As we cycled slowly towards the finish line, I glanced back at my daughter and smiled. Then I treated her to a personalised rendition.

'Edith, Edith, give me your answer, do. I'm half crazy all for the love of you. It won't be a stylish marriage, I can't afford a carriage. But you look sweet, upon the seat, of a bicycle made for two.'

Jumping Someone Else's Train

'These tube trains are lethal,' I said, as the doors slammed shut behind us, nearly severing Frank's trailing foot. 'We could easily get separated from each other, or the kids could get separated from us.'

'We'll be fine,' Frank said. 'You worry too much.'

'We should at least have a plan for if we lose each other. Can you imagine how it would be if we lost our children on the Xi'an Metro? I would never forgive myself. And we might never find them again.'

'Sounds blissful.' I elbowed Frank in the ribs.

Both Frank and I lived in London when we were younger, so we spent a lot of time on the Tube. If someone got trapped in the doors we were used to them opening up again. But the Chinese subway system was completely different. As soon as the buzzer sounded, the doors slammed shut like a clam, and they were not going to reopen. You were either in or out. Or you were travelling through the tunnels with one of your limbs stuck in the door. There were no half measures.

'Listen up, kids,' I said as the train we were on swept smoothly through the tunnel. Alfie and Edith looked vaguely in my direction. 'I said, "Listen up!" This is important.' This time it came out as a teacher style growl. The kids turned towards me and finally made eye contact.

'If we ever get separated on one of these trains, then you get off at the next stop and you stay exactly where you are. You do not move from that spot until we come to get you. Do you understand?'

'Okay, mum,' Edith said. Alfie muttered a vague 'Yeah'.

'I said, "Do you understand?"' I used my best 'don't mess with me' teacher voice. The kids nodded meekly. I felt sure that the message had gone in.

After another busy day of sightseeing in Xi'an, it was time to get back to our hotel. As we made our way down the stairs in the metro station, a train was arriving at the platform.

'Jump on!' I ran towards the train. Alfie raced ahead with me, Frank and Edith following behind him.

Alfie did as instructed, running through the doors and into the train. I was close behind him, but as I went to get on the doors slammed shut in my face. There was a moment when time seemed to stand still. Alfie was on the train. Frank, Edith and I were on the platform. My nightmare scenario had come true. I held my hand up to the window of the train and mouthed desperately to Alfie, 'Get off at the next stop and wait for us!' Alfie smiled at me, wandered off down the train and slumped into a seat. He didn't seem especially concerned.

As we waited for the next train to arrive, my heart was thudding in my chest. What if Alfie didn't get off at the next stop? What if we got to the next stop and he wasn't there? How was I ever going to find my son again?

'Do you think he'll be alright? Do you think he'll remember to do what we agreed?' There was a slight tremble in my voice.

'You worry too much.' Frank said. 'He'll be fine.'

The five minutes before the next train arrived seemed to take forever. Eventually a train swept into the station and we piled on board. As we waited to depart, an elderly couple rushed down the stairs onto the platform and hurried over to the train. The woman made it on board with seconds to spare, but the man was a bit slower. The train doors slammed shut when he was only partway through. The man was wedged half in, half out of the train. The woman grabbed the man's arm and tugged hard. The man didn't move. She tugged harder still.

Eventually, just as the train seemed sure to depart with the man stuck in the doors, he finally popped inside. Our short journey to the next station was punctuated by the sound of a blazing row between the pair. Even though we didn't understand a word of what they were saying, it wasn't hard to get the gist.

'Why did you rush onto the train, you stupid idiot?'

'It's not my fault you got stuck in the doors, you fool!'

The train whizzed through the tunnel to the soundtrack of the elderly Chinese couple arguing. Eventually it slowed as it came into the next station. As the train ground to a halt I looked out of the doors, desperately searching for the sight of my son. But the platform in front of us was completely empty.

'What do we do?' I turned to Frank in terror. 'Where is he? What if he stayed on the train? How do we know where he is? How will we ever find him?'

'Don't panic,' Frank said. 'Let's get off and have a look.'

As soon as the doors slid open, I rushed off the train, dragging Edith behind me. I wasn't planning to lose her as well. There was an empty space on the platform in front of me where Alfie should have been. My heart thudded in my chest. I felt my stomach drop. I looked desperately up and down the platform.

And then a wave of relief flooded over me. Halfway down the platform, our son was sitting on a bench, looking supremely unconcerned. He had his head down and he was reading his book.

I raced down the platform and tried to sweep Alfie up into my arms. 'I didn't know where you were!' A sob caught in my throat. 'I was so worried. I thought we had lost you forever!'

'Hang on a sec, mum,' Alfie fended me off with one hand. 'Just let me finish reading this page.'

Army Dreamers

No trip to China is complete without a visit to the Terracotta Army. The huge army of warriors, horses and archers was created to guard over the body of the first emperor of China, Qin Shi Huang. They remained buried for over 2,000 years, until some farmers stumbled upon them by accident in 1974 when they were digging a well for water. We had been dreaming about our visit to the Terracotta Army since the day we first decided that we would come to China. What we hadn't yet figured out was how we were actually going to get there.

The hotel lobby was full of signs advertising different excursions in and around Xi'an. We could go and see the Terracotta Army for $150 a head, or we could see the Army and the nearby Huaqing Pool and Lintong Museum for $200 a head. But our plan was to take more of a 'do it yourself' approach (or, as Frank would say, 'do it yourself more cheaply' approach), which had been our attitude during our entire Road School adventure.

It was early morning when we headed to the bus station, which was conveniently situated just a few blocks away from our hotel. I'd like to claim credit for this, and say that I had honed my accommodation booking skills over the course of the six months of Road School, but actually it was just a happy accident. We had been worrying for a couple of days about whether we would be able to find the right bus to take us to see the warriors. As we rounded the corner into the depot, which was located at the side of the train station, we saw that we needn't have worried. There was a line of buses with distinctive decals on them showing images of the warriors. It didn't seem to matter which bus we picked, so we hopped onto the nearest one, paid the fare of a few yuan and settled in for the ride. Everyone on the bus apart from us was Chinese – despite the decals, this was definitely not a tourist ride.

An hour later we pulled up in a large car park, having stopped at every single bus stop between Xi'an and our destination. Only a handful of people were left on the bus. We got off and followed the line of other visitors heading towards the entrance to the tombs. As we walked through rows of stalls selling replica warriors of all different shapes, sizes and materials, the sellers called to us to buy their wares. We ignored their calls – we could buy souvenirs later. We had an army of terracotta warriors to see.

Just as we reached the entrance to the tombs, the heavens opened and it began to pour with rain. We bought our tickets and dashed over to the huge hanger that covered the first vault that had been excavated. We stepped into the foyer and shook the water from our clothes. And then we pushed through some glass doors and into the main hanger.

It was impossible to do anything but gasp in amazement. In front of us, and looking directly at us, were row after row of life-sized terracotta soldiers, over a thousand of them in total. It felt as though an entire army was marching towards us. Edith stood there staring. Her mouth had dropped open.

'Wow. Just wow,' she said.

Alfie came to stand beside her. 'Amazing.'

Frank joined them. 'It is pretty impressive, isn't it?'

I came to stand with my family and we gazed into the vault together, marvelling at the soldiers lined up in their ancient majesty, guarding the tomb of their emperor. It was amazing to think that these figures had been hidden underground for 2,000 years, that they had been discovered by accident and that we were lucky enough to be here at this moment, seeing them in real life. It was nothing less than a dream come true.

Downtown Train

After sampling the delights of the bullet train from Beijing to Xi'an, we were going to travel from Xi'an to Shanghai on the Z train. The Z train took slightly longer than the bullet train to make the journey, but it was about half the price which made Frank very happy indeed. We were going to travel overnight, taking the 'soft sleeper' option, and that meant that we would get a cabin to ourselves – with beds. I had never been on a sleeper train before, and I was really looking forward to the experience. It felt to me like there was something rather romantic and nostalgic about travelling through the night on a train.

Xi'an train station was hot and crowded. After we had dragged our suitcases through a strict security check, we headed into the busy station. We slumped into a row of plastic seats and tried to make sense of what it said on the information boards. The Chinese characters swam in front of my eyes.

'Do you know what Shanghai looks like when it's written in Chinese characters?' I said to Frank. I was a bit nervous that we might miss our train.

'Nope.'

'Do you think we'd better find out?' Frank headed off to make some enquiries.

Eventually we found what we hoped was the right waiting room, and we piled up our luggage in a corner to wait for our train to arrive. We had come well prepared for the night. We had lots of snacks. We had plenty of reading material. But most importantly of all, we had three bottles of wine and two glasses.

The train arrived. We hurried on board and trailed through the train with our suitcases until we found our carriage. It was compact but it was comfortable enough. We all bundled inside and made ourselves at home. With the top bunks down, the carriage was completely full. Edith and Alfie lay down on the top bunks, opened their books and settled down to read. Frank and I lay down on the bottom bunks. Frank yawned. We all looked out of the window as the train set off from Xi'an on its long journey to Shanghai.

'Fancy a drink?' Frank said, wiggling his corkscrew at me.

'It's only 4 p.m.'

'Yeah, but we've got three bottles to get through. Why don't we make an early start?' Frank popped open the first bottle, poured two glasses, handed one to me and we settled in for the ride.

'Are you two drunk?' Alfie said, a couple of hours later.

'Nos rilly,' Frank slurred.

'Nos in the slighest,' I hiccupped. 'Open the nest boddle, Frank. And gimme a kiss.'

Frank leaned over and gave me a big wet kiss. Alfie and Edith looked at us in horror. And we both burst into an uncontrollable fit of the giggles.

Going Underground

The Huangpu River splits Shanghai in two. On one side of the river is the Bund, an attractive riverfront walkway lined with buildings from the days of colonial Shanghai. The locals like to stroll along the wide pavement taking in the views of the Pudong skyline on the opposite side of the river. You can cross the river on the metro or you can take a boat across it. But part of today's plan was to take the trip across the river through the Bund Sightseeing Tunnel. My Eyewitness guidebook had promised that it was part subway ride, part fairground haunted house, and an experience that was definitely not to be missed.

An escalator took us underground towards where the Bund Sightseeing Tunnel began. On either side of us, murals of underwater scenes made it feel like we were descending into the depths of the sea. We bought our tickets at a kiosk and then we headed over to the entrance. A silvery carriage with huge windows pulled up in front of us. It looked like something out of a space age movie. We stepped into the carriage and the door swished shut. Then it set off with a lurch.

Some strange sounds came out of the speaker in the corner of the carriage. It sounded like we were underwater. Eerie jingly-jangly music played, exactly like something from a fairground. As we moved forwards, golden lights flashed around the tunnel ahead of us. They moved faster and faster until they looked like some kind of wormhole. I began to feel distinctly dizzy. Then a disembodied voice replaced the weird music.

'Basalt buried in the ocean,' a male voice said, or at least I think that's what it said. Blue lights flashed in circles as the carriage progressed slowly through the tunnel.

'What buried in what?' Alfie looked at me. I shrugged.

There was more weird music, more weird lights. When the guidebook promised that this was the most surreal and kitsch thing you could do in Shanghai, it definitely wasn't wrong.

'Mass of magma,' the voice said, as the lights turned red. A female voice repeated the phrase in Mandarin.

Next came some strange noises that sounded like people in torment. The narrator warned us that this was 'paradise and hell'. There was an evil laugh. Then the jingly-jangly backing track changed to a softer, childlike music. Strange figures came at us out of the darkness. The disembodied voice kept going, but by this point I had given up trying to make any sense of what it was saying. I was mainly praying that it would all be over soon, even though the ride was only a few minutes long in total.

'Basalt in blue water,' the voice came through more clearly now. A little bit more jingly-jangly music, some watery bubble sounds.

'Meteor shower,' said the voice, and there were some more flashing lights. And then, thankfully, we were done. We stumbled out of the carriage, looked at each other in complete and utter confusion, and then headed back up the escalator into the light.

Parklife

We stood at the windows of our apartment hotel in Shanghai, transfixed by what we were seeing. Off in the distance, in the dark night sky, someone was flying a kite. The kite was lit up, and it bobbed and weaved like a diamond dancing through the darkness.

'The Chinese invented kites,' Edith said. 'Tomorrow I want to fly a kite.'

'We'll have to buy a kite first. And find a park to fly it in.' I flicked through the pages of my guidebook. 'Here you go, Lu Xun Park looks like our best bet. They have a boating lake as well. It should be fun.'

As we exited the metro at the Hongkou Football Stadium station, we still hadn't had any luck in finding a kite. Edith was in a right grump about it.

'You promised me you would buy me a kite,' she said, as we went up the escalator that took us out of the station.

'Look!' I said, pointing at a little old lady who was squatting on the pavement outside the metro station. In front of her was a rug laid out with lots of children's toys. And one of the things she was selling was kites.

'Hurrah!' Edith said, and she hurried over and started inspecting the kites, eventually picking out a rainbow coloured one. Frank did a quick bit of bargaining, and got Edith her kite. She clutched it tightly against her chest and smiled broadly at us. It was the perfect weather to fly a kite – there was enough of a breeze to get a kite up in the sky, but not so much that it would be tricky to fly it. Edith skipped the rest of the way to the park.

At the entrance to Lu Xun Park was a large sign listing all the things that were prohibited in Lu Xun Park. Halfway down the long list was a picture of a kite.

'Noooo!' Edith threw her brand new kite to the ground in disgust.

'We'll take it back to England with us and we can fly it there,' I said.

Despite the lack of kite flying opportunities, inside the park there were all sorts of things to keep us entertained. First, we hired a couple of pedal driven rickshaws to take a tour of the park. These were far more exhausting to drive than they looked, so after a quick circuit we handed them back in at the hire kiosk. Next destination was the lake to hire a boat for another boating adventure. Frank ducked out of this one, on the basis that last time round he had nearly capsized the boat and had got soaking wet. He lay down on the grass for a snooze while I took the kids out for a spin on the lake.

'This park is great,' Alfie said, as we docked our boat and clambered out. We started to make our way towards the exit.

'Look at that!' Edith said, pointing into the distance. 'I want to go on that pirate boat!'

I blinked and did a double take. There seemed to be a large fairground in the park. It had dodgems, one of those swinging boat rides where you sail high in the air, countless merry-go-rounds and a train track elevated on stilts that ran right around the perimeter. The fairground was completely deserted. It felt like we had fallen asleep and woken up after a zombie apocalypse.

'Why is there no one here?' Alfie looked around the fairground.

'Maybe it's not open yet.' I said. We walked in through the gates. There was a man sat in a kiosk. We went over and pointed to the pirate boat swing. The man pointed to a price list. We handed over a payment for two tickets, and then the kids scrambled on board and strapped themselves in. The man hit a button and the boat began to swing from side to side. The kids whooped and screamed with delight as the boat rose higher and higher in the air, until they were almost upside down.

'That was amazing,' Alfie said, stumbling off the boat and over to us.

'I don't care about not being able to fly my kite any more!' Edith said.

'This place is brilliant.' Alfie looked around at the deserted rides. 'Can we go on the dodgems next?'

A View to a Kill

'A hundred and twenty yuan?' Frank said, reading from the tariff board outside the Jin Mao Tower. 'I'm not paying twelve quid each to get a view of Shanghai. Especially since we're going to be in the clouds when we get up there.'

I looked upwards, craning my neck to see the top of the silvery skyscraper. Frank was right. The sharp point at the top of the tower had disappeared into the clouds.

'There is an alternative,' I said, studying my guidebook. 'The Shanghai Grand Hyatt Hotel is inside the Jin Mao Tower, and apparently there's a breathtaking view from the hotel reception on the fifty-sixth floor.'

'We're not staying at the Shanghai Grand Hyatt Hotel though, are we?' Frank pointed out.

'Well, we can pretend that we want to take a look at it. With a view to staying there for a night.'

Frank looked at me with a sceptical expression on his face. He was wearing a scruffy t-shirt and jeans. His t-shirt had sweat stains under the armpits from a day of traipsing around in the Shanghai heat. I looked equally dishevelled. My jeans were stained. The shirt I was wearing, which I hadn't bothered to iron that morning, was crushed from a day of sightseeing. The kids were dressed in t-shirts and tracksuit bottoms.

'We don't exactly look like the kind of people who would be able to afford a night in the Grand Hyatt Hotel, do we?' Frank pointed out.

'No, but I'm great at bluffing. Follow me.' I headed towards the entrance.

A doorman dressed in a smart suit and a top hat opened the door to the Jin Mao Tower and made a kind of bowing motion. Our untidy little family trudged inside.

'Wow!' Alfie said, gazing around him at the gold painted walls and the high ceiling. 'This is well posh.'

'Keep up,' I said, heading to the back of the foyer where there was a bank of four lifts. I pressed the call button and the doors swished open in front of us. We stepped inside the luxurious lift. It had golden walls and a giant full length mirror on one side. I pressed the button for floor 56 and the doors swished closed. The lift ascended swiftly and silently.

When we arrived at the fifty-sixth floor, we stepped out into a large atrium style room. Glass windows edged the space giving a stunning view of the whole of Shanghai. The foyer was full of business people dressed smartly in expensive looking suits. Women in traditional Chinese costumes were gliding around serving expensive looking drinks. The reception desk was off to our right, so we darted out of the lift and turned left.

'Quick,' I said. 'Let's have a look at the view and get out of here.'

We lined up against the glass wall and took a few minutes to admire the view of Shanghai that was laid out in front of us, marvelling at how the other half lives. Then we got our grubby, scruffy selves the hell out of there and headed back to our budget hotel.

Money, Money, Money

One of the things you learn very quickly when you spend time in China is that, even if you really don't want to bargain and you are happy to pay full price for something, you are still going to have to haggle for it. If you don't bargain, it is as though you are insulting the shopkeeper's soul. One time, Frank even ended up having to negotiate for some bottles of wine in a Chinese supermarket. He not only got a 30% discount off his purchases but also a free corkscrew.

As our time in Shanghai drew to a close, the children were desperate to buy a few more souvenirs to take home with them, so we had come to the Yu Gardens and Bazaar, a famous shopping area. Edith wanted to buy a Chinese lantern to hang in her room and a golden waving cat. Alfie wasn't sure what he wanted to buy, but he was sure that he would find something. Frank and I had consulted, and we'd decided that it was time for the children to learn how to bargain by themselves. This would be maths in action. First up it was Edith's turn to buy herself her golden waving cat.

She went into the shop, picked up the cat that she wanted, turned it over and nodded. 'This is the one I want,' she said with a tone of certainty in her voice.

I took it from her and inspected it. 'Are you sure? This is tat, really, isn't it?' Inside a cheap plastic case was an even cheaper looking plastic cat. It was painted gold and its paw waved at me as I held it. 'How much is it?'

'It's fifteen yuan,' she said. 'How much is that in English money?'

'Well, there are ten yuan to the pound,' Frank told her, 'so you work it out.'

'It's £1.50 then. That sounds fair.' She unzipped her purse and fished inside for some money.

'Remember to bargain,' Frank said, as the shopkeeper approached. 'Don't let him know that you really want it or you'll have to pay more.'

'You want?' the shopkeeper said to Edith, pointing to the cat.

'I'm not sure,' Edith said, replacing the cat and chewing on a fingernail.

'Atta girl,' Frank muttered out of the side of his mouth.

'Is very good cat,' the shopkeeper said, picking up the cat and thrusting it towards Edith. 'Very good price, too.'

'How much is it?' Edith said, with a steely look in her eye.

'Fifteen yuan,' the shopkeeper said.

'It's too expensive,' she said, putting the cat back down.

The shopkeeper picked it up and gave it back to her. 'I do special price for you.'

'I'll give you ten yuan,' Edith said. 'And not a single yuan more.'

I looked at Frank. He looked at me and raised an eyebrow. Our daughter was impressive at this. We should have taken her with us when we bought that wine.

'Twelve yuan,' the shopkeeper said.

'Too expensive,' Edith told him. She replaced the cat once more, turned on her heels and hurried out of the shop. We all trailed after her.

As we walked away down the street, the shopkeeper came hurrying up behind us. He had the plastic waving cat in his hand.

'You pay ten yuan,' he said, holding the cat out to her.

Edith stopped, raised an eyebrow and smiled at Frank.

'No thanks. I only want to spend eight yuan now.'

The shopkeeper grimaced. Then he nodded.

We went back into the shop and Edith bought her plastic golden waving cat for eight yuan. I didn't feel too bad for the shopkeeper, though, because by the look of that cat it probably hadn't cost more than 8p to manufacture.

Next it was Alfie's turn. Alfie umm-ed and ah-ed. He still wasn't sure what he wanted to buy. That is, until he saw the chicken.

'I want to buy this,' Alfie said, calling over to me. He was holding up a hideous rubber chicken.

'Why on earth do you want to buy that?' I said.

'Because it does this,' Alfie said. He squashed the chicken's belly and a hideous noise came out of its mouth. The noise was somewhere between a cock crowing and a badly injured person groaning. I had a sudden image of a baggage handler leaning on our suitcase as he loaded it into the plane and *that* noise coming out of it.

'How much is it?' Frank said.

'It's twenty yuan,' Alfie said, pointing to the sign.

'You're going to have to haggle,' I pointed out to Alfie.

'Sis?' Alfie said. Edith turned to him. 'Could you get this for me? You're really good at bargaining.'

As we headed back to our hotel with a carrier bag full of tat, Edith couldn't wipe the grin off her face.

'Did you see how I bargained him down to nine yuan for that rubber chicken?' she wanted to know. 'Did you see how I good I was at getting the best price?'

'You're a natural,' Frank said, a proud smile on his face. 'Maybe you should be an accountant when you grow up.'

'I'd love that daddy,' Edith said. 'I love numbers.'

'Like father, like daughter,' Frank said, smiling proudly. 'Now, have I ever shown you how to work a spreadsheet?'

Land of Confusion

'We're just going out to get some food at the supermarket,' I said to Edith and Alfie. 'Would you like to come with us or stay here?'

'Can we stay here?' Alfie said. The kids had flopped on the sofa. They were exhausted after a busy week in Shanghai and the five and a half hour bullet train ride back to Beijing.

We had just arrived at a managed apartment block on the north-west side of the city. We were treating ourselves for the last week of our trip. The apartment was the most luxurious one we would stay in during our entire visit to China – there were two large bedrooms, two bathrooms and a huge lounge and kitchen area. Frank was looking particularly happy at the idea of having separate bedrooms. The apartment block also had a swimming pool. But since we had only just arrived here, the cupboards were completely bare. And so, even though it was dark and late and we didn't know this part of Beijing at all, we were going to have to venture out in search of food and drink.

'Okay,' I said. 'We won't be long. We'll be back in an hour or so.'

The kids had turned on the TV and were busy flicking through the channels in search of something that they really shouldn't be watching.

'Don't worry about them,' Frank said. 'They'll hardly notice that we're gone.'

We made our way down to the reception desk and asked about the location of the nearest supermarket. The receptionist marked an X on the tiny map that we had been given on our arrival at the apartment block. Then we stumbled out into the sticky night air. According to the map, the supermarket was close by – maybe ten minutes' walk at the most. This should be no problem at all. We would get a few bits and pieces and hurry back to our fancy new apartment to cook dinner and relax. What could possibly go wrong?

The supermarket was easy enough to find. We followed the map and walked past tower blocks and neon signs which flashed bright

Chinese characters into the sultry, humid air. Eventually we found a huge shopping mall filled with every kind of shop you might expect to find in a typical Western shopping centre. We headed through the shopping centre and across a road, all the time following signs for the supermarket. Eventually we were directed into an underground warren of shops. We wound our way past stalls selling all manner of exciting Chinese delicacies. Finally we arrived at the supermarket. A vast escalator took us upwards. We split up the list between us and headed off into different sections to gather our supplies. This was easier said than done, since the store was huge. Thirty minutes later, though, we reconvened at the tills and paid for our shopping.

'Now, which way is out?' I said to Frank, looking up and down the length of the checkouts.

'Well, we came in that way,' Frank said, pointing to our right, where we could see the massive escalator that had brought us up and into the supermarket. 'But the sign says the exit is that way,' Frank said, pointing to our left. We were trapped in a one-way system. The only way out was in the opposite direction to the way we had come in.

'I've got a bad feeling about this,' I said to Frank as we followed the sign towards the exit. I was already disorientated after walking through the maze of underground stalls. I had no idea which way was which.

'You worry too much,' Frank said. 'It'll be fine. Once we get outside it will be obvious which way to go to get back to the apartment.'

The exit signs led us up and back out into the heat of the night. We both stood there, looking around us. The exit from the shopping centre had brought us out on the side of a main road. I had never seen this road before in my life.

'It's this way,' Frank said, heading off to his right. He sounded pretty sure, so I trudged after him, the handles of the carrier bags digging into my hands. After walking for five minutes, Frank stopped. I caught up with him and dumped my bags on the ground, then I shook my hands to try to get some blood back into them.

'Which way now?' I said.

'Err,' said Frank.

'What do you mean "err"? Are we lost?'

'No, we'll be fine,' Frank headed back in the direction we had just come from. 'It must be this way.' I picked up the carrier bags and trotted after him.

'Let's try this way,' I said, taking a left turn away from the main road. 'That tower block over there looks familiar.'

An hour later, we had tried heading in every different direction to relocate our apartment block. We had shown our map to several confused looking Chinese people, and been given several different sets of directions. We were both sweating. The carrier bag handles were cutting deep grooves into my palms.

'We're lost, aren't we?' I said.

'I'm sure we'll find it soon,' Frank sounded more hopeful than convinced. 'It's probably just around that corner,' he said, pointing in the direction from which we had just come.

'Right, that's it,' I said, coming to a halt. 'I'm fed up with this. I'm starving hungry. It's sweltering hot. These carrier bags are killing my hands. And the kids will be desperately worried by now. I'm getting a taxi.' I waved at a passing cab. The cab driver drove on without stopping.

'You can't get a taxi,' Frank said.

'Why on earth not?'

'Because we're probably only a few hundred yards away. It'll be totally embarrassing. And a waste of money.'

'I know that, but we might as well be a few hundred miles away for all the chance we have of finding it again. I am not bloody going a single step further.' I'd had enough.

After five failed attempts, I finally found a taxi that was willing to stop. He didn't have much choice but to stop, since by this point I was standing in the middle of the road trying to flag down someone, anyone, who could return us to our apartment block. We dumped our carrier bags in the boot and slipped gratefully inside the air-conditioned taxi. The seats felt wonderfully comfortable after two hours of trailing around in the oppressive heat.

The taxi driver turned around and looked at us as if to ask 'Where to?' I handed him the tiny map on which the receptionist had marked an 'X' as we set off on our 'quick trip to the supermarket' over three hours earlier. The taxi driver said something in Mandarin, which I imagine was something like, 'You must be kidding – it's just round the corner,' then he set off at top speed. Thirty seconds later we screeched to a halt outside the apartment hotel building. Frank handed him a bundle of yuan and we retrieved our shopping from the boot.

'Thank god for that,' I said, knocking on the door to the apartment. Edith opened it. We stepped inside and dumped our carrier bags on the floor.

'Where have you *been?*' Edith wailed.

'What have you been *doing?*' Alfie shouted.

'I'm so sorry, children,' I said. 'We got lost. You must have been desperately worried.'

'No,' said Alfie, 'we weren't worried, we were watching the TV. They have cable TV here so we've been watching *River Monsters* and *Ice Road Truckers.*'

'But we're *starving!*' Edith opened up one of the carrier bags and scrabbled around inside. 'What did you get for dinner?'

Union of the Snake

While seeing the Terracotta Army and visiting the Great Wall were at the top of my 'things to do in China' list, top of Alfie's list was to 'eat some unusual creatures'. And the best place to do this, according to the guidebook, was at the Donghuamen night food market in Wangfujing Street.

We strolled down the street, watching as the vendors set up their stalls. They were opening up large metal barbeques and filling them with coals. Alongside each barbeque were trays containing a selection of weird and wonderful creatures on wooden sticks. There were scorpions, spiders, seahorses and snakes. All ready to be put on the barbeque, as soon as someone ordered them.

'That's disgusting!' Edith said. 'I feel sick. I'm not going anywhere near those stalls once they start cooking that stuff.'

'It looks great to me,' Alfie said. 'I'm just not sure which one to choose.'

'We'll wait here,' I pointed to a bench at the end of the row of stalls, 'while your dad and your brother go and choose what they want to eat.'

Frank headed off down the line of stalls with Alfie. Ten minutes later they were back. Alfie was chewing something on a stick.

Whatever it was it looked revolting.

'It was a tough choice,' Alfie chewed away at the gristly looking piece of meat on a stick. 'It was hard to decide between the spiders and the scorpions. But in the end I went for snake.'

It's my turn to choose a meal,' Edith announced the next day. 'And I want a roast chicken dinner tonight.'

'I'm not sure they even do chickens here,' Frank said. Edith started to cry.

'It's not fair. Alfie got to eat a snake. Now I want to eat a roast chicken.'

'We can have a look in the supermarket,' I said. 'I'll go and see what I can find.'

An hour later I got back from the supermarket and dumped a carrier bag on the table. 'This is the best that I could do.'

And so it was that that night we feasted on roast chicken, although 'feasted' is not quite the right word. The Chinese chicken wasn't exactly like the chickens you find in the UK. This chicken was the size of a partridge, and by the time I had burnt it to a cinder in the oven, it had barely enough meat on it for a couple of mouthfuls. But that didn't seem to matter to Edith.

She pushed her empty plate away, turned to me, wiped her mouth and sighed contentedly. 'That was the best roast chicken I have ever eaten.'

'It was a bit burnt,' Alfie said, letting out a loud burp. 'And whatever they tell you in the books, chicken doesn't taste anything like snake.'

You Spin Me Round (Like a Record)

'Let's sit down over there and take a rest,' Frank pointed to an area of Tiantan Park off to our right. There were some picnic benches next to lots of adventure style play equipment – balance beams, wheels to spin, exercise bikes and even a set of uneven bars. The kids dashed off and began to play. Frank and I flopped down in the shade to have a drink.

'This is great!' Edith shouted over to us, as she swung her way across a set of monkey bars. She dropped to the ground and then went over to try the balance beam.

I took out my guidebook and studied it. We had come here to visit the famous Temple of Heaven, one of the largest temple complexes in China. It was right in the middle of this large, lush, beautiful green park.

'Come and help me with this one, dad!' Alfie shouted over to Frank. Alfie was holding on to the handle of a giant wheel. On the other side of the wheel was a group of small Chinese boys chatting away excitedly in Mandarin. As they tried to push the wheel around one way, Alfie pushed it back with all his might in the other direction. The group of boys was winning easily against Alfie. Or at least they were until Frank went over to join in. Frank grabbed the handle alongside Alfie and put all his strength and weight behind it. The boys didn't stand a chance. Frank was at least twice as tall as them and twice as wide as well. They pushed and they pushed, but they just couldn't get the wheel to turn with Frank holding on to it. More and more Chinese boys joined the group, until there were at least ten of them doing battle, but still Frank and Alfie held the wheel firm. The loud, animated chatter of small boys drifted across the park towards me as they tried to beat the two Westerners.

As I watched the men of our family prove their strength, I

noticed a teenage boy arrive at the park and make his way over to the uneven bars. He put down his rucksack, unzipped it and took out some gloves. He put the gloves on and took a moment to compose himself. Then he jumped up and grasped hold of the tallest of the bars and hung there for a moment. Suddenly, he began to swing, his legs kicking out in front of him, then behind him, gaining more and more momentum. Eventually he was going fast enough to swing his body right the way over the top of the bars. Around and around he spun, gaining speed all the time. One by one, people in the park stopped what they were doing and began to watch. Then, just when I felt sure that he couldn't spin any faster, the boy let go of the first bar. There was a collective gasp from the spectators. The boy turned a full somersault in the air, and moments later he caught hold of the second bar.

Now he was really getting going. He did a series of different spins. A one armed spin, a spin with a twist, around and around he went until I felt quite dizzy. Reaching the top of an arc, he paused, in a handstand position, his toes beautifully pointed and his body perfectly straight. Seconds passed. Still he held the handstand. Then again he dropped down and spun around and around the bar, picking up speed as he turned and twirled. He swung off the lower bar, somersaulted and caught back hold of the first one. Another handstand, a few more spins and twirls, a final push off the bar, a double somersault in the air, and then he made a perfect landing on the ground. He clicked his heels together, took off his gloves, put them back in his rucksack, dusted down his hands and headed off. The people who had been watching the display went back to what they were doing.

'Did you see that boy, mum?' Edith said, hurrying over and settling down in the shade next to me. 'He was awesome.'

'He was amazing, wasn't he?'

Frank staggered over to where we were sitting, rubbing his upper arms as though he was in pain; Alfie trailed behind him, shaking his hands as he came.

'Did you two see me and Alfie beat those boys?' Frank said.

'Which boys?' I said.

'The ones on the other side of the wheel. There were loads of them but they couldn't turn the wheel with Alfie and me holding on to it. We're super strong, aren't we, Alfie?'

'Yeah, we were like super heroes,' Alfie agreed, flexing his arm muscles.

'Err, Frank,' I said. 'We weren't watching you and Alfie.'

'You weren't watching us?' Frank sounded aghast. 'Why on earth not?'

'Because we were too busy watching that other boy do an Olympics style gold medal quality gymnastics display on the uneven bars.'

Frank scratched his goatee and looked puzzled. 'What gymnastics display?' he said.

Don't Get Me Wrong

After years and years of dinosaur obsession, Alfie knew the names of pretty much every dinosaur that had ever been discovered. He knew whether they were carnivores or herbivores. He knew which one was the biggest and which one was the smallest. He knew what size they were and what kind of claws they had. He knew where and when they lived, and for how long. And he knew when something wasn't right with a dinosaur exhibit.

The Beijing Museum of Natural History was located just outside Tiantan Park, so it was perfectly situated for a visit after we had been to see the Temple of Heaven. After a quick look around the main section of the museum, we headed for the Dinosaur Park, which apparently featured animatronic dinosaur models. We were hoping for a similar experience to the vast and impressive dinosaur exhibit at the Natural History Museum in London, particularly the bit where you go around a corner and a giant full size T-rex roars at you. However, we had been unwise to get our hopes up.

'That model of *Tyrannosaurus rex* is all wrong,' Alfie passed judgement in disgust. 'It's completely the wrong size. And it didn't move like that at all.'

He walked over to the next exhibit and stared at it, a look of disbelief on this face. 'That *Iguanodon* has the wrong head on the wrong body. And where is its thumb claw?' He shook his head.

'Now this one,' he said, pointing to a *Coelophysis*, 'this one is *almost* right. But it would never have been in the same location as that *Stegosaurus*. The *Coelophysis* lived in the Triassic period, while the *Stegosaurus* lived in the late Jurassic. And it is completely the wrong size.'

Edith pressed a button and the model dinosaurs in the exhibit wiggled around a bit and made a sound. Unfortunately the sound they made was more like a cat being strangled than how you might imagine a dinosaur would roar.

'Can we get out of here now?' Alfie said. 'I don't think I can take any more of this.'

Don't Bring Me Down

Figuring out which part of the Great Wall of China to visit, and how to get there, took a fair bit of doing, and a lot of time on the TripAdvisor website. Apparently some parts of the wall were far too busy, with so many tourists that we would barely be able to squeeze our way along them. Other parts of the wall were too far from Beijing for a day trip, or were broken and treacherous to traverse. But Mutianyu – now that sounded promising. Mutianyu was not too busy. Mutianyu was within driving distance of the capital. And Mutianyu not only had a cable car that would take us up to the wall, but it also had a toboggan ride that would bring us back down again. Hard as I tried to visualise what these two things could possibly be like, I found it impossible. A cable car and a toboggan run? In China? It just didn't make any sense. This wasn't the Alps. This was the Far East.

'We're going up *there*, on *this*?' Frank said, gulping.

Frank is what you might call a big guy. He doesn't do all that well with delicate things. He once broke a glass coffee table just by sitting on it, which could have been extremely painful, although thanks to the safety glass was merely extremely embarrassing.

We were in the queue for the cable car that would take us up to the Great Wall of China. Calling it a cable car would have been a breach of the Trade Descriptions Act, if they had such a thing in China. This cable car consisted of an open bench seat suspended from some thin looking wires. The mechanical parts of the cable car looked almost as ancient as the wall itself. Up ahead of us we could see people making the long slow ascent to the wall, dangling perilously on the open seats. Between where we stood at the base station, and where we would reach the wall, there was a massive drop to the ground, hundreds of metres below. If you can imagine crossing the Grand Canyon sat on a broken park bench suspended from a piece of fraying string, you will get somewhere close to what we were about to do.

'You'd better go with Edith, and I'll go with Alfie,' I said. If we could minimise the total overall weight on each cable car, perhaps the string wouldn't break like that glass in the coffee table did.

'I'm not sure about this,' Frank groaned.

'Next!' said the cable car guy.

I jumped onto the seat and Alfie hopped in alongside me. We pulled the bar down and our journey began. As we made our way across a vast open chasm, we could see across to the toboggan ride below us. Metal toboggans raced their way down through a series of twists and turns on a metal track. Excited as I was about getting up to the Great Wall of China and going exploring, I was even more excited about riding that toboggan run back down.

I twisted around on the seat to look behind me to see how Frank and Edith were doing. And I immediately wished that I hadn't. The bench on which they were sat was tilted precariously to one side. Frank was a good foot lower than Edith. Frank had his eyes shut and appeared to be praying. Given Frank's atheism, this was pretty worrying to see.

'What were you thinking?' Frank said, as he stumbled off the cable car. His face was ashen and his entire body seemed to be shaking.

'Coward,' I said. It was nice not to be the one who was most frightened for once.

'Loser,' said Alfie, laughing at how white his dad's face had got.

'That was fun, dad!' Edith was oblivious to her father's pained expression. 'Can we do it again?'

Wonderwall

The mortar between the blocks on the Great Wall of China is a striking white colour. People used to believe that this was because it was made of the ground up bones of the workers who were forced to build it. But recently they found out that, actually, it is white because it contains ground rice, which is very sticky and therefore makes a particularly good mortar.

'Now I'm in China,' Edith said, doing a little dance routine, 'and now I'm in Mongolia!' She stuck her arm out of the north side of the wall. 'Or at least my arm is!' Of course, her arm wasn't *actually* in Mongolia because the Great Wall does not run along the modern day border between China and Mongolia. But I kind of got what she was thinking because the wall was originally built to keep out the Mongol hordes. And I didn't like to spoil her fun in my quest for geographical accuracy. We could always look at a map later on and get to the facts of the matter.

'It's very hot up here,' Frank wiped the sweat from his brow.

'It's very steep up here, too,' I said, as we trudged up yet another steep section of wall towards one of the guard turrets that were dotted along its length. The views into the far distance were stunning. There were mysterious shaped mountains to the north of the wall and a hazy view across fields towards Beijing to the south. The air was hot and humid. Thankfully, we had remembered to bring the children's rainbow umbrella sun hats.

'I want to take some photos!' Alfie grabbed the camera from my hands and began snapping away.

'But I wanted to go first!' Edith folded her arms and pouted.

'You can take it in turns,' I said. 'Five photos each and then swap over.' Alfie was already busy snapping away in all directions. 'Make sure you both get some good pictures, though,' I warned them. 'This is a day we'll want to remember.'

The Great Wall of China was surprisingly steep. I suppose I shouldn't really have been surprised at this, since it is built on the top of some very high mountains. But I wasn't quite expecting it to go up and down in quite such an up and down way. We slogged slowly up an almost vertical section, pausing every few minutes to catch our breath and wipe the perspiration from our foreheads. The hot Chinese sun that had finally emerged from the smog baked down on us relentlessly.

'Did you know that the Great Wall of China *isn't* actually visible from the moon?' Alfie said, as we sat resting in the shade of one of the guard towers. 'It's just a myth.'

'No way,' I said. It sometimes seemed like we were learning as much from our kids during Road School, as they were learning from us.

After a few hours exploring the wall we were exhausted. It was time to head back down via the heavily anticipated toboggan run.

'I hope you got some good photos,' I said to the kids.

'Oh yeah, sure,' Edith said.

'No problemo,' Alfie added.

That evening, when I uploaded the photographs that the children had taken, there were several photos of Alfie's trainers, an equal if not slightly greater number of pictures of Edith's sandals, a large number of images where the edge of a rainbow sun hat obscured part of the view. And one solitary uninterrupted image of the Great Wall of China.

Here Comes the Rain Again

If the cable car up to the Great Wall was terrifying, the way down looked like it was going to be one of the most exhilarating experiences of our lives. A long silver toboggan run snaked its way down the side of the mountain, steep and curving. The metal gleamed in the afternoon sunshine. We watched as one by one people set off in their toboggans down the gleaming track.

'This looks amazing!' Alfie said.

'I can't wait!' said Edith.

We handed in our tickets and took our places on a toboggan each, waiting for our turn. Frank was first, with Alfie second, Edith third and me coming up the rear. The man at the front was letting people go, one after the other, with a few seconds in-between each toboggan. There were signs everywhere warning us to control our speed and to leave sufficient space between each person. We edged slowly forwards towards the 'Go' sign.

Frank gave a whoop of delight and set off, closely followed by Alfie and then Edith. I could see them racing quickly down the track. I let the brake off my toboggan and made it to the front of the line, ready to follow the rest of my family down the run. Then the man controlling the queue held up a hand. A frown passed across his face. He looked up at the sky where a nasty looking black cloud had suddenly appeared.

'You wait!' he said.

'But … but … my children!' I said, pointing to where Alfie and Edith had disappeared down the hill just moments before.

'You wait,' he said, looking at me sternly and holding up a palm in the internationally recognised signal for 'STOP'. He started shouting up to a man who was positioned higher up the slope on a platform looking back up towards the Great Wall. They were both paying a keen interest in a knot of dark, swollen clouds that had drifted over the wall. The bright sunshine suddenly disappeared and a fat drop of rain plopped down onto the track in front of me. I gulped. I didn't fancy the idea of being stuck on a metallic track, in a metallic toboggan, in a thunderstorm. If there was lightning, this metal track was going to act as the world's most efficient conductor. And if there was rain, the track was going to turn into a lethally slippery surface. I started to wonder if I was ever going to get down from the Great Wall. I looked across to where the cable cars were still cranking their treacherous way up to the wall. I didn't fancy their chances in the event of a tropical storm either.

The shouted conversation between the two men continued. Behind me, I could hear muttering from the line of other tourists, trapped in their toboggans. Another drop of rain splashed onto my head. Then another. Ten minutes later, the heavy grey cloud finally drifted off into the distance and the sun came back out again. By this point, the tourists waiting in their toboggans were beginning to murmur about staging a rebellion. The man finally indicated that I was free to begin my journey down. I took my foot off the brake and sped away. With a clear track in front of me, I could go as fast as I wanted to.

'Where have you *been*?' Edith said as I heaved myself out of my toboggan and tottered away on unsteady feet.

'You will not *believe* what happened,' I said. 'There were a few drops of rain and they kept me waiting at the top until it stopped. So I had the entire toboggan run to myself. I went really, really fast. It was brilliant.'

'Just wait until you hear what daddy did, though,' said Alfie.

'What did you do, Frank?' I looked at him with suspicion.

'He totalled the guy in front of him.' Alfie was all excited. 'He smashed into his toboggan, and the guy went sailing through the air. Boom! Bang! Smash! Whee!'

'Frank?' I said.

'There was this American guy in front of me,' Frank explained. 'I kept catching him up, so I braked and slowed right down. But then I got to this straight stretch and he was nowhere to be seen, so I barrelled down it at top speed. But what I didn't realise was that there was a bend at the bottom. And as I came round the bend, in front of me was this guy, at a complete standstill, because the people in front of him had stopped to wait for the people in front of them.'

'Tell mum what happened next, dad,' Alfie said.

'Well, there was nothing I could do,' Frank said, warming to his story. 'I smashed straight into him. Kapow! He flew up into the air and his toboggan went flying off down the track. So he was lying there on his back, sprawled across the track. And then Alfie came steaming round the corner behind me as well. Well, if Alfie had hit me with his toboggan, I would have hurtled forwards and crushed the guy with my toboggan. So this poor guy jumped to his feet, scurried over to his toboggan and went zooming off as quickly as he could.'

'Frank,' I said, 'I sincerely hope you apologised.'

'I did try when we got to the bottom,' Frank said, 'but the guy just said, "No worries, dude," and hurried off as fast as he could. I think he was a bit freaked out. He's probably heading to the hospital to get treatment for whiplash as we speak.'

I shook my head. So it wasn't the rain that was the most dangerous thing on the toboggan run that day. It was Frank. We headed off down the hill towards the exit just as the heavens opened. We needed to find our driver and get the hell out of there, before the American guy returned with questions about his medical bills.

Relax

The *Rough Guide to China* said that the aqua park at the Beijing National Aquatics Center was not to be missed, and the *Rough Guide* wasn't wrong. The kids looked in through the window and gasped in amazement. The massive space where the Olympic swimming events had taken place was filled with over a dozen different slides. There was a huge beach-shaped pool in the centre filled with smiling swimmers. We paid our entry fee, got changed and passed through a foot dip into the park. Just as we arrived, the clock struck the hour and music began to blare out of the speakers. A siren sounded and a voice announced that a typhoon was about to hit the beach. The wave machines ground into action as hundreds of Chinese people raced off the slides and into the water.

Our family are old hands at aqua parks. We know exactly what it's like to swim in a tsunami of pee. What usually happens when we go to an aqua park is that the boys go on every slide, and are particularly drawn to the most dangerous or terrifying ones. If Alfie takes a liking to a certain slide, he will go up the stairs and down the slide at least thirty times. Meanwhile, Frank will be busy figuring out a way to subvert the slide. He will go down it backwards or take up the position that guarantees him maximum speed. When he reaches the bottom, he exits in spectacular fashion, positioning his body so that he skims across the water like a stone, spraying any unsuspecting spectators with a sheet of water.

Edith and I, on the other hand, prefer to lie in the sun, read books and eat snacks. Once we are sufficiently warmed up we will go on a couple of slides and then declare that we are 'a bit chilly' and that we should go and lie in the sun again to warm up. We will spend the entire day doing a few of the slightly less dangerous or terrifying slides, while building up to going on the most dangerous or terrifying one. Finally, we will climb up the stairs to the most dangerous or terrifying slide together, clinging on to each other as we go. We will peer over the edge, look at each other and decide that we might just give it a miss after all. After that we will return to our default position of lying in the sun and eating snacks.

'C'mon, this looks fun!' I grabbed Edith and Alfie and raced into the water, swimming out to where the waves were biggest. Gradually, the wave machines built up to maximum force and we were flung about from side to side. Eventually, the waves calmed down and stopped, and everyone headed out of the pool and back to the slides.

'Let's see what's up there first,' Frank said, pointing to a massive staircase to the left of the beach. We climbed up three flights of steps and reached the top. Ahead of us was the entrance to the most terrifying looking water ride that I had ever seen. A sign with English translation told us the ride was named 'The Tornado'. At the start of the ride was a pool full of water. In the pool sat a giant inflatable ring which seated four people. As we waited in the queue, we watched as people sat down on the rings, gripped on for dear life and were pushed into the mouth of the ride, where they immediately disappeared out of sight. I could just make them out further down the ride, plunging down alarming looking drops and hurtling round corners at speed.

'I am not doing this,' I said as we neared the front of the queue.

'I am!' said Edith.

'I am!' said Frank.

'I am!' said Alfie.

We edged forwards. I felt as though I was heading towards a fate worse than death. My stomach churned. We reached the front of the queue. The couple in front of us got onto the ring, one on either side, leaving two spaces free.

'You too short,' the attendant indicated Edith. Edith stepped to one side, a disappointed look on her face.

Frank stepped forward. The attendant looked him up and down once, then he slid a pair of scales in front of him and indicated that Frank should step onto them. Frank got onto the scales and the needle spun round as far as it could go. (Chinese scales are clearly made for weighing Chinese sized people, not Frank sized ones.)

'You much too fat,' the attendant said, indicating to Frank to step aside.

'You just right,' the attendant said, indicating to Alfie to sit down on the giant inflatable ring.

'That's great then – off you go Alfie. Enjoy!' I shoved him towards the ring.

'He must go with partner,' the attendant said. 'Must have four people on ring.'

'Ah,' I said.

'You just right too. You partner,' the attendant said. Then he indicated that I should sit opposite Alfie on the ring. I was left with no choice. I lowered myself in and grabbed the handles.

'We'll wait for you at the bottom. Good luck!' Frank winked at me. Then he and Edith headed back down the stairs.

'If I make it,' I said, and steeled myself for the ride.

Something that I have learned over the years, from life in general and also from going on both rollercoasters and water slides, is that if you tense up it feels a million times worse than if you just let it happen. This is probably a good rule of thumb for most things in life. As the attendant pushed our giant ring towards the entrance to the ride,

I forced myself to relax.

At first the ring eased its way gently down the slide, but as it turned a corner I could see a vertical drop directly ahead.

'Relax, relax,' I whispered to myself.

'Are you okay, mum?' Alfie said.

'Oh yes, I'm fine,' I smiled.

'You're very pale.' Alfie sounded concerned.

The ring dropped like a stone, leaving my stomach behind. I had just recovered from the shock when the ring spun round, dropped again and spun again, swooshing its way through the water. We drifted towards another vertical drop. I could see a massive tube shaped bowl ahead of us. The ring plummeted suddenly and sped up the side of the bowl, until we were hanging almost upside down in the air. Then it dropped again and sped up the other side of the bowl. By this point I was ready to puke. The ring did its side-to-side motion several more times, accompanied by the sound of my terrified screams.

Then, finally, the ring came out into a flat stretch of water. Frank and Edith were waiting for us at the end of the ride. When the ring stopped moving I heaved myself up and staggered away, clutching my stomach and taking deep breaths. My nerves were shattered.

'You don't look so good,' Frank said.

'I don't feel too good,' I said.

'Did you enjoy it?' Edith said.

'It was great fun!' Alfie said. 'C'mon, mum, let's do it again!'

Homeward Bound

Even though we had been in China for nearly a month, and bargained our way to lots of souvenirs during that time, Edith and I still had one last purchase to make. Clothes. Unfortunately, though, we had left it to the very last minute. We were hoping there would be some good shops at the airport, and luckily we weren't wrong.

'How about this one?' Edith said. She held up a tiny silk dress in front of her and did a twirl.

'It's lovely, but I'm not sure it's going to fit you.' The clothes seemed to have been created for the tiniest of tiny Chinese people, not for our full size English frames.

'What about this one?' Edith held up a dress that was at least five sizes too big.

'Too big. We'd better hurry up and buy something, then we can go and find daddy and Alfie. We don't want to miss our flight.'

Edith finally settled on a pale purple silk dress, with a label that said it was for someone four years older than her. I chose a long silk coat and a silk bag.

'Is it time to get our flight yet?' Edith said, as we made our way over to where Frank and Alfie had been waiting outside the shop. Frank had a disgruntled look on his face.

'It's been delayed,' he said. 'Four hours.'

'Great!' Edith said, grabbing my hand and dragging me back into the shop. 'We can go and do some more shopping!'

Four hours later, and a few hundred pounds lighter, we finally boarded our flight to Moscow.

'Will they have shops at Moscow airport, daddy?' Edith said, as we settled into our seats.

'I would imagine so,' Frank said. 'Why do you ask?'

'Because I want to buy one of those Russian fur hats, and I definitely need a Russian doll.'

Frank looked at me with a grimace on his face. 'I'll tell you something for nothing. My wallet is going to be glad when we finally get home.'

Chinese Lessons

1   When you visit the East, having been brought up in the West, the experience is palpably different. The food, the buildings, the language, the landscape, the people – pretty much everything feels like the polar opposite of what you are used to at home. (Unless the hotel you are staying in happens to have a Belgian bar.)

2   There is no point in visiting another country and getting cross because the people don't behave in the same way that people do back home. The Chinese attitude to spitting, queuing and shopping irritated us at times, but that was our problem, not theirs.

3   Road School was not just about a philosophy of education; it was also about a philosophy of parenting. Ironically, one of the aims of spending more time with our children was to encourage them to gain in confidence and to become more independent from us.

4   There is a balance between keeping your children safe and letting them develop their independence. Travel is a great way to explore this balance, because it gets children used to coping with change, difference and difficulty.

5   To get a proper feel for geography, and for what our big wide wonderful world is like, you should definitely travel.

6   Trying new and different foods is exciting, but there are times when only the cuisine of your home nation will do. (Even if your home nation is Britain.)

7   The Chinese have a knack for creating great visitor attractions. Sometimes they were kitsch; sometimes they were terrifying; sometimes they were breathtaking. But one thing is for sure – they were never boring.

8   Souvenirs are a great reminder of a trip to a foreign country. They are like breadcrumbs that you pick up on your journey, so that you can retrace your steps when it is over.

9   You can save a lot of money by organising your own travel. The only thing we actually had to do via a tour company while we were in China was book train tickets.

10 If you don't take a few risks in life, you will never know what could have happened.

A Road School Curriculum

In 1988, a national curriculum was introduced in state schools in England, Wales and Northern Ireland. The national curriculum laid out what children should learn at different stages in their schooling. Although it has evolved over the years, and is no longer statutory for certain types of school such as academies, the national curriculum has filtered its way into the nation's consciousness. It has come to represent a set of knowledge that every child *should* learn. In the United States, the introduction of the Common Core State Standards Initiative in 2009 was a similar attempt to specify the curriculum that everyone should receive.

The national tests, GCSEs and A levels that students sit serve to reinforce the idea that there is a specific set of knowledge which equates to 'an education'. However, when you are home educating, it is *entirely up to you* what and how you wish to teach your children. Or, rather, what and how you wish your children to learn. You might choose to include part or everything that is in the national curriculum, or you might not.

When you 'plan' your curriculum:

- Remember that teaching is not the same thing as learning. You don't have to teach your children directly for a set number of hours each day in order to educate them.
- Bear in mind that you are not the only available source of knowledge and expertise. If your child can read, they might learn as much from reading a book about a topic as they do from you giving them a lesson on it.
- Take into account how learning can happen simply by visiting a place and exploring it. Don't feel that you always have to formalise your visit by turning it into a 'lesson'. The experience of going somewhere can be memorable and educational in its own right.
- Tourist sites often have a strongly educational element built into them, with signs, information boards, interactive exhibits, etc. Further opportunities for learning may be available on the website associated with the site and through leaflets and other printed materials available during your visit.
- Involve your children in making decisions about the content of their

curriculum, particularly when it comes to choosing topics or themes. What would they most like to study during your learning journey together? You can teach subjects such as English or history through cross-curricular 'themes' rather than as discrete lessons. Ask your children to decide which topics interest them the most and capitalise on those.

- ⛵ Remember that learning can take place all the time, and anywhere, rather than just during 'school' hours. It doesn't matter what time of the day or day of the week it is – if there is learning happening, then your child is being educated.
- ⛵ Much of what your children will learn on the road is social and emotional rather than intellectual. They learn how to cope, how to adapt, how to be resilient and how to be brave. The challenges and difficulties that you face on the road will teach them all these things without any direct 'teaching' needed at all.
- ⛵ One of the great things about educating your child yourself is that you get to learn alongside them. Not only do you provide a model of lifelong learning, but it's also very liberating to learn new things as an adult.

English

Our children had learned how to read and write at school, and they were both already keen readers, so planning for English was about giving them opportunities to read, write and talk. When you are planning for learning in English:

- ⛵ Consider how you will transport reading materials. We took paperback books with us, rather than electronic ones, because we prefer to be hands on with our reading.
- ⛵ We allocated one of the suitcases as a 'portable library' completely filled with books, supplementing it as we travelled.
- ⛵ Take a mix of fiction and non-fiction books. We left the storybooks behind us when we had finished with them for someone else to find and read.
- ⛵ Think ahead about the topics that your children might like to read about after you have visited specific places and take materials on these with you. There are many fantastic reference books available – the Dorling Kindersley range is particularly good.
- ⛵ Souvenir shops at big tourist attractions often offer an excellent

selection of books on related topics and in a range of languages. There was a particularly good bookshop at the Colosseum. We inadvertently ran out of books in China, but luckily we found a great English language bookshop in Shanghai.

- Getting our children to write in their diaries worked really well – it gave a structure to the day, ensured that they wrote regularly and encouraged them to reflect on what they had learned.
- Remember that English can be about all kinds of communication. We encouraged the children to be inventive in how they completed their diaries – for instance, adding drawings, tickets, notes, doodles and numbers as well as words.
- Encourage the children to write postcards and letters to friends and family at home, telling them all about their adventures on the road.
- Speak at an adult level with your children, using words that they might not have previously encountered, such as 'philistine', 'connoisseur' and 'claustrophobic'. Make your conversations a source of learning for vocabulary.

Maths

Maths was everywhere on our road trip. It was in the money we used, the distances we travelled, the time we got to each place and how long it took us to get there. It was in every cry of 'Are we there yet, daddy?' In school, maths follows an increasingly abstract pathway, like most subjects. The more complex the theory gets, the further the subjects move away from concrete, real world scenarios.

To find maths in everyday situations with your children:

- Buy them wallets and give them spending money of their own. Encourage them to make decisions and choices around money and to manage a small budget.
- Talk about the prices on menus and encourage your children to figure out how much you are going to spend and how much change they would get from different amounts.
- Explain how currency exchange works and get them to work out the value of items in different currencies – for example, converting from yuan to sterling.
- Ice cream is great as a motivator for understanding money – if your children want ice creams, give them a handful of coins and insist

that they get their own. Buying ice creams is also an effective motivator for encouraging them to speak in different languages.

- Study the money that passes through your hands – what images or symbols are on the coins and notes, and what does this tell you about the geography or history of a country?
- The coins in the eurozone specify their country of origin, which very handily links maths learning to geography.
- If you travel to a different time zone, this gives you a great opportunity to talk about how and why times differ according to where you are in the world.
- Work out the distance you have travelled during each stage of your journey, in both miles and kilometres.
- Use different forms of travel to explore maths – discuss the speed you are going in a car/plane/metro/bullet train and how this relates to the time taken to travel to your destination.

It is fun to create some mental maths games, based on your children's interests, to play while you are on the move. For instance, we played 'Minecraft Maths' whenever we were on a metro or subway. I would call out a multiplication or division puzzle, featuring blocks or characters from Minecraft, then the kids would race to answer it. Frank's job was to figure out whether their answers were correct or not.

Science

The natural history museums, zoos and aquariums we visited were brilliant for learning about science. We saw a fantastic range of exhibits, and entry was often cheap or free for the children.

To plan for scientific learning on your travels:

- When you visit a museum, take some time to identify the exhibits you would like to see. You might base this on your children's favourites, or you might feel that you need to fill in some gaps in their learning by seeing something new.
- Ask questions as you go around a zoo or museum – for instance, get the children to find out which continents the different animals come from.
- Take books on scientific subjects such as birds, volcanoes, weather, landscape, rocks, crystals and minerals.

- Take field guides to help you identify the animals and plants that you see in each location.
- Keep an eye out for interesting rocks, shells, bones and other natural items as you walk around – children are very drawn to these 'found' objects, and they make a great resource for learning.

Most of the hotels and apartments we stayed at had cable television, giving us access to good documentaries for learning. The children loved any wild animal ones, particularly the *River Monsters* programmes.

Geography

Being on the road is essentially one extended geography lesson. Although you can learn about the countries of the world from a book or from your teacher, there is nothing like actually visiting them to really get to know them. When you move between countries, you start to create a mental map of how they all join up together.

To make the most of the opportunities for geographical learning:

- Study atlases and globes before you go to give your children a sense of the overall journey you will be making.
- Take lots of guidebooks and maps with you, including simpler ones that will be accessible for your children.
- Sometimes, when you are exploring somewhere on foot, put your children in charge of the map reading and see what happens.
- Talk about the points of the compass and link this to learning about the sun and the stars.
- Pick up leaflets and booklets at the sites you visit and use these as texts for further learning.
- On planes, there is often a 'flight map' that shows where you are as your flight progresses. This is a great visual aid for helping your children to map the journey conceptually.

History

The world is dotted with historic sites. As you travel around visiting them, you can go back in time to the days of the Ming dynasty or the fall of the Berlin Wall. One of the great joys of our trip was creating a kind of 'grand tour' of famous sites.

To plan for historical learning:

- Read up yourself, before you go and while you are travelling around, so that you can help your children understand more. Guidebooks contain lots of detailed information, including historical details. I would read these in the evenings so that I was one step ahead of the children.
- Encourage your children to imagine what the places you visit would have been like when they were first built. Get them to recreate the atmosphere in their imagination. Talk about how places would have felt from the viewpoint of different people – a Roman Emperor or a slave in the Colosseum, for instance.
- Create a visual timeline and, related to the sites you visit, show your children when in the course of history different events took place.
- Link the historical events that were going on in one country you have visited with those that were happening elsewhere at the time – for instance, talking about what was going on in Europe at the time of the Ming dynasty.
- Many sites have people dressed in historical costumes as a way to impress the tourists – we saw Ming warriors at the city wall in Xi'an and Roman soldiers at the Colosseum. Take the chance to talk with your children about what people wore, what it was made of and why.
- Keep an eye out for historical artefacts – we found some fascinating pieces of tile on the edge of a lake and pieces of animal bone on a beach.

Physical education

Although you might not be able to do too much in the way of organised sports while you are away, we found lots of other ways to stay active:

- Hiring bikes is a great way to get around – our bicycle tour of the walls in Xi'an was a real highlight.

- Tourist sights are often fairly close together – in Rome, for instance. If you walk from one to another you can potentially walk several miles in a day.
- We climbed a lot of stairs during our trip – up and down to several top floor apartments and up and down various towers.
- Combine relaxation with fun by going swimming, whether it's in the sea, at an aqua park or in a lake or river. Several of the hotels we stayed in had swimming pools which meant we could have a relaxing swim after a hard day's sightseeing.

The arts

A highlight of our trip was our visits to numerous art galleries, and seeing lots of art and sculpture in museums as well. Several of the modern art galleries we visited were free to enter. You can also find lots of public art and sculpture on the streets, as well as fascinating architecture, particularly that of cathedrals and other religious buildings.

To plan for artistic and cultural learning:

- Talk to your children about which paintings, sculptures and buildings they like, and get them to articulate why it is that they like them. Encourage them to be specific about what makes an artwork 'good' in their eyes.
- Hunt together for the symbolism and imagery that is often hidden away in paintings and sculptures. What do the children think these symbols might mean?
- Discuss the way that paintings give us an insight into the history of the time – the clothing, the attitudes (e.g. to women and children), the religion and the food.
- Identify how the architecture differs from country to country, and consider what this might say about the culture and the materials available locally.
- Pick some famous artists to trail, especially if you are touring around Europe. You can find examples of the work of artists such as da Vinci and Michelangelo in a number of different countries and locations.

When you visit historical sites, you begin to see how drama, theatre and performance would have played a key part in people's lives in the past.

Places like the Colosseum give you a powerful sense of the kind of spectacle they would have encountered first hand.

We were lucky enough to visit a number of different theatres on our journey, including the Large Theatre in Pompeii, built in the second century BC, which seated around 5,000 spectators; the Theatre of Syracuse in Sicily, where they were setting up for a theatre festival when we visited; and the underground Goethesaal, in the caves of the Harz in northern Germany, which is used as a venue for modern day performances. If you get the chance, it is a lovely idea to take your children to some live shows while you are travelling.

Modern foreign languages

When you travel you are surrounded by other languages, and you start to understand how important and useful it is to be able to communicate to people in their own tongue. You also gain a sense of how different the sounds of languages in different parts of the world are. Travel helps children to understand that, despite speaking different languages, we are all essentially the same under the skin. To support your children's MFL learning:

- Take a mini phrasebook and learn to use a few phrases and some vocabulary in each of the countries you visit.
- Practise counting to ten in different languages.
- Buy newspapers and magazines in other languages for your children to explore and examine.
- Let your children hear you trying to speak in other languages, especially if you don't find it easy. Set them an example to help them build confidence.

Beyond the curriculum

While you might plan for learning in each of the separate subjects, one of the great things about home educating your children is that you can move beyond the traditional curriculum boundaries. The individual subjects get intertwined and mixed up together because of the way you are learning. If your child wants to do a project on Leonardo da Vinci, that project can encompass learning in many different subjects – art, maths, design, geography, history – all these and more can be drawn out as you explore his life together.

Although our personal situation does not allow for us to home educate long term, and our children are now happily settled back into school, it was a brilliant experience to move beyond the curriculum and learn on the road for a while. And who knows? Edith has just started in Year 6, and I have offered her the option of home schooling again to avoid SATs. Perhaps it is only a matter of time before we set off on our travels again.

Epilogue

Home At Last

We shuffled through passport control at Heathrow and out into the baggage reclaim area. Our eyes were red, our hair was long and our clothes were filthy. But we were nearly home. Just the luggage to collect, and then we could get out of the airport and back on the road to Somerset. It was strange but lovely to be back in a world where all the signs were in English, rather than in Chinese characters, and where the people around us were speaking in a language we could understand.

Our flight number came up on the overhead screen and we limped across to baggage carousel number four. The wheels on the trolley I had picked kept steering me over to the right. It was good to be back home, I thought, where even the trolleys had a mind of their own. A crowd of our fellow passengers gathered around the conveyor belt. They all looked exhausted. They stood in silent expectation of getting their suitcases back and getting the hell out of there. The belt began to turn. At first it circled empty, then bags started to rise up from the depths and emerge one after another through the black flaps. People stepped forward to claim their belongings.

'Is that ours?' Edith pointed at a black suitcase.

'Not that one,' I said.

'Is that ours?' Alfie pointed at a multi-coloured suitcase.

'Nope.'

'Is that ours?' Frank pointed at another black suitcase.

'Our one has got a pink ribbon on it so it's easy to recognise,' I said, taking a moment to congratulate myself on my forward planning.

The luggage carousel went round and round, a single red suitcase making the circular journey every minute or so. The other passengers from our flight had long since come and gone. The kids had long since given up hope. The belt ground to a halt.

'Uh oh,' Frank said, 'this doesn't look good.' We plodded over to the lost baggage desk, where a short queue of fraught looking passengers waited, frowns on their faces.

'It looks like your bags are in Moscow,' the customer service agent said. He didn't look all that bothered about our predicament. 'They must have missed the transfer. They'll arrive on the next plane.'

'When's the next plane?' Frank said.

'This evening.' The customer service agent shoved a form in Frank's direction. 'Fill this out and we'll get them delivered to you when they arrive.'

'Oh well, it's only stuff,' I said.

Everyone nodded. We were too exhausted to care. We trudged off, tired but happy, to pick up our car. Road School had been an incredible adventure. We'd had the most amazing experience of our lives, but luggage or no luggage, it was time to go home.

Your Road School ...